Brand-New from Ripley's!

The astounding team from Ripley's has done it again—and what a job they've done. Strange, startling, weird and wonderful, these oddest of oddities from the remotest corners of the globe are as fascinating as they are fantastic—and, of course, every single one is true!

Did you know that—

- A parrot saved the life of Leo, son of Emperor Basil of the Byzantine Empire, who was about to be executed by his father, because the parrot had been trained to cry "Poor Leo"—Emperor Basil spared his son and Leo became ruler of half the Roman world—880!

- The dessert served by King James V of Scotland to each guest at a banquet consisted of a deep dish filled with gold pieces!

- "Noowomantamooonkauunonnash" in the language of the Algonquin Indians means "love!"

- Sally Mutton of Bristol, R.I., was pronounced dead in 1900, but her husband refused to accept the doctor's statement—and held off the undertaker with a shotgun. He poured hot milk between his wife's lips—and she regained consciousness and survived her husband by 40 years!

Ripley's Believe It or Not! titles

Ripley's Believe It or Not! 28th Series
Ripley's Believe It or Not! 29th Series
Ripley's Believe It or Not! 30th Series
Ripley's Believe It or Not! Ghosts, Witches and ESP
Ripley's Believe It or Not! Great Disasters
Ripley's Believe It or Not! Stars, Space and UFOs

Published by POCKET BOOKS

Most Pocket Books are available at special quantity discounts for bulk purchases for sales promotions, premiums or fund raising. Special books or book excerpts can also be created to fit specific needs.

For details write the office of the Vice President of Special Markets, Pocket Books, 1230 Avenue of the Americas, New York, New York 10020.

Ripley's Believe It or Not!

29th SERIES

PUBLISHED BY POCKET BOOKS NEW YORK

Another *Original* publication of POCKET BOOKS

POCKET BOOKS, a division of Simon & Schuster, Inc.
1230 Avenue of the Americas, New York, N.Y. 10020

Copyright © 1978 by Ripley International Limited

Published by arrangement with Ripley International Limited

ISBN: 0-671-46216-4

First Pocket Books printing November, 1978

10 9 8 7 6 5 4 3

POCKET and colophon are registered trademarks
of Simon & Schuster, Inc.

Printed in the U.S.A.

PREFACE

While the number 29 may not have the flash and dazzle of some more showy numbers (The "Twenty-Nine" Commandments? Tea for twenty-nine?), still it must have its points—countless women all over the world elect to remain twenty-nine for years.

Now this discreet, self-effacing figure has something new to celebrate—the book you have in hand is twenty-ninth in the *Ripley's Believe It or Not!* series. And in keeping with our custom, we'd like to pay a little homage now to the number of our latest edition.

It was October 29, 1929, that the stock market crashed, the Dow Jones plunging 122 points!

It was November 29, 1926, that the United States Supreme Court upheld the "Dry Law" prohibiting whiskey consumption except with a doctor's prescription.

In was in 29 A.D. that Jesus Christ was crucified, according to calculations by Dr. Oswald Gerhard of Berlin.

And November 29, 1886, was the day travelers in Scranton, Pennsylvania, climbed aboard the first electric streetcar to collect fares!

Lest 29 came to connote calamity and bother, we might add that 1829 marked the arrival of the original Siamese twins in Boston on August 16. Chang and Eng, joined together at the waist, struggled for 63 years to live their separate lives. Both married and fathered a total of 22 children.

And, of course, it was in 1829 that the first reference to baked beans appeared in a book entitled *The Frugal Housewife*. Finally, it was in 1929 that the Ripley's Believe It or Not! feature was syndicated worldwide!

With that, we bid you welcome to our 29th collection of fascinating people, places, and things, all of them fun to read about, and all of them *absolutely true*—Believe It or Not!

Ripley International Ltd.
Toronto, Canada

Ripley's
Believe It
or Not!®

THE **HIGHEST** GOLF COURSE
IN THE WORLD
Cerro de Pasco, Peru,
14,300 FEET
ABOVE SEA LEVEL

A **HARP** POPULAR IN 18th Century Europe **WAS PLAYED BY A KEYBOARD**

EZRA WESTON II
of Duxbury, Mass.,
LEADING SHIPOWNER IN THE U.S.
IN THE MID-19th CENTURY

WAS SO INFLUENTIAL AND
POWERFUL HE WAS NICKNAMED
KING CAESAR II

NATURAL CRUCIFIX

Church of Maria Strasengel, Austria —
A PLANT THAT GREW IN THE SHAPE OF A CRUCIFIX

ANDREA CONTARINI
(1296-1382)

ELECTED DOGE OF VENICE, THE HIGHEST POST IN THE REPUBLIC, 3 TIMES REFUSED TO ACCEPT THE HONOR—UNTIL HE WAS ORDERED TO ASSUME IT **UNDER PAIN OF DEATH!**

HE SERVED AS DOGE FOR 14 YEARS

A **PARROT** SAVED THE LIFE OF LEO, SON OF EMPEROR BASIL OF THE BYZANTINE EMPIRE, WHO WAS ABOUT TO BE EXECUTED BY HIS FATHER, BECAUSE THE PARROT HAD BEEN TRAINED TO CRY "**POOR LEO**"

EMPEROR BASIL SPARED HIS SON AND LEO BECAME RULER OF HALF THE ROMAN WORLD
880

THE REV. ARTHUR WAGNER
(1850-1902)
of Brighton, England,

CONSTRUCTED 5 CHURCHES IN THAT COMMUNITY AT HIS OWN EXPENSE - SPENDING HIS ENTIRE FORTUNE OF MORE THAN $375,000

ANTONIO BIENVENIDA
famed Spanish bullfighter

IS THE SON AND GRANDSON OF MATADORS, NEPHEW OF 3 MATADORS, AND BROTHER OF 2 MATADORS

RAMPSIDE HALL
near Barrow-in-Furness, England, WAS BUILT WITH 12 CHIMNEYS —

SO EACH OF THE OWNER'S 12 SONS COULD HAVE A ROOM WITH A FIREPLACE
1608

NUTTALL'S POORWILLS COUSINS OF THE WHIPPOORWILL *HIBERNATE*

THE **AARDVARK** SPENDS THE DAY UNDERGROUND IN TUNNELS, *EMERGING ONLY AT NIGHT*

FRANÇOIS EPERVIER of Paris, France, WAS SO CERTAIN THE RULE OF EMPEROR NAPOLEON III WOULD BE BRIEF THAT HE VOWED HE WOULD DRINK A GLASS OF WATER *EVERY HOUR OF NAPOLEON'S REIGN* HE ACTUALLY DRANK A GLASS OF WATER EVERY WAKING HOUR *FOR 18 YEARS !*

The **YOUNGEST FATHER**

Richard Michael FATHER

WAS BORN ON FATHER'S DAY Albany, N.Y.

12

THE DESSERT
SERVED BY KING
JAMES V of Scotland
TO EACH GUEST
AT A BANQUET
*CONSISTED OF A
DEEP DISH FILLED
WITH GOLD PIECES*

MRS. **MARTHA WALDO LINCOLN**
THE MOTHER OF 2
NEW ENGLAND GOVERNORS,
GAVE 3 SUCCESSIVE SONS
THE FIRST NAME OF WALDO
*-AND SAW ALL 3
DIE IN INFANCY*
SHE THEN GAVE HER
NEXT TWO BOYS WALDO
AS THEIR MIDDLE
NAME —AND BOTH
SURVIVED TO MANHOOD

**THE MOST INACCESSIBLE
CEMETERY IN THE WORLD**
Douzes, France
*A GRAVEYARD LOCATED ATOP THE
GREAT ROCK OF SAINT-GERVAIS
700 FEET ABOVE THE JONTE RIVER*

MANY POST OFFICES
in East Bengal,
Pakistan,
TO BETTER SERVE
THE POPULACE
*ARE LOCATED
ON BOATS*

LINCOLN DRUGS
in Oak Park, Mich.,
HAS A TELEPHONE NUMBER
THAT SPELLS OUT ITS NAME
LI 3-7847
(D RUGS)

THE FIRST ORANGE TREE IN ITALY
PLANTED IN THE GARDENS OF
SANTA SABINA, ROME, IN 1216
IS STILL GROWING 746 YEARS LATER

"NOOWOMANTAMOOOONKAUUNONNASH"

SAY IT
AGAIN!

IN THE LANGUAGE OF THE
ALGONQUIN INDIANS
MEANS "LOVE"

LADIES in Purang, Tibet, USE ONLY ONE COSMETIC —*SOOT!*

THE MEETING HOUSE GRAVEYARD in Old Sturbridge Village, Mass., IS FULL OF AUTHENTIC TOMBSTONES —*YET IT DOESN'T HAVE A SINGLE GRAVE*

THE
REVOLVING ROCK
Trancoso, Portugal,
A **BOULDER** WEIGHING **30** TONS,
SO DELICATELY BALANCED ON
ITS NATURAL STONE PIVOT THAT
THE *ROTATION OF THE EARTH
SPINS IT HALFWAY AROUND
EACH DAY !*

CHRISTIAN SCHMALZ
of West Hempstead, N.Y.,
HAD
8 CHILDREN
8 GRANDCHILDREN
8 GREAT-
GRANDCHILDREN

THE
REV. THOMAS COLE
MINISTER OF
LIZARD POINT,
England,

WALKED
26 MILES
IN ONE
DAY TO
VISIT A
SICK
PARISHIONER
*WHEN
HE WAS
120
YEARS
OF AGE*

AN **OFFICIAL PROCLAMATION** SEALED WITH WAX IS POSTED OVER CROPS in Purnea, India, **TO FRIGHTEN AWAY INSECTS**

HORN-SHAPED SEA SHELLS ARE USED BY CHILDREN in India **AS SPINNING TOPS**

BEER IS BREWED BY the Nyoro Tribe of Bunyoro, Africa, BY MIXING COOKED BANANAS WITH SWEET GRASS AND WATER **AND STAMPING ON IT FOR HOURS WITH BARE FEET**

MEXICAN BEAN MARKED BY NATURE WITH A PERFECT **5**
Submitted by MRS. LYDIA DAVILA, Los Angeles, Calif.

17

FORT ERIE and **LAKE ERIE** WERE BROTHERS IN PHILADELPHIA, PA.

THE LIVING GATE

ENTRANCE ARCH TO A TEMPLE in Osaka, Japan, *FORMED BY 2 TALL TREES*

PHEBE RIPLEY (1742-1825) of Concord, Mass., WHO DIDN'T BELIEVE IN WASTING TIME, TAUGHT LATIN AND GREEK TO A CLASS OF HARVARD STUDENTS *WHILE PEELING POTATOES WITH HER HANDS AND ROCKING A CRADLE WITH HER FEET*

18

AN OAK TREE STANDING IN EASTON LODGE PARK, near Dunmow, England, FOR 1,000 YEARS, WAS DYING IN 1944 UNTIL A WORLD WAR II BOMB DUMP EXPLODED NEARBY— *IT HAS FLOURISHED EVER SINCE*

THE **REV. JOSEF BÖCK** (1804-1900) WAS A PASTOR IN Guntramsdorf, Austria, *FOR 74 YEARS*

THE **MOST AMAZING POLITICIAN IN ALL HISTORY** FENG YAO (881-954) Prime Minister of China, RETAINED HIS POST **THROUGH 9 REVOLUTIONS!** *HE SERVED UNDER 10 EMPERORS AND 5 DIFFERENT DYNASTIES*

19

COINS

ONCE WERE MADE IN
the Chad Territory,
Africa,
**FROM BROKEN
PIECES OF POTTERY**
*THE MORE JAGGED
EDGES THEY HAD
THE GREATER
THEIR VALUE*

CAN YOU DISTRIBUTE
THE DIGITS FROM
1 TO 9 IN THE SMALL
CIRCLES
*SO THAT EACH LINE
ADDS UP TO 15 ?*

John, EARL of WORCESTER

1427-1470
SENTENCED TO DEATH IN LONDON, England,
AS ATONEMENT FOR HIS
MANY ACTS OF CRUELTY
*ORDERED THE HEADSMAN
TO TAKE 3 STROKES*

MEN OF THE ODDE CASTE
Kanara, India,
ARE THE ONLY MEN IN THE WORLD
WHO **SHAVE WITH MILK!**

THE
LADY CHAPEL of Ely, England,
WAS CONSTRUCTED IN 1321 BY
JOHN of WISBECH, A MONK, WHO
FINANCED ITS CONSTRUCTION WITH
*A TREASURE CACHE
HE HAD FOUND
ON THE SITE*

A
CHIEF'S TOMB
In the Danakil Desert of Ethiopa
IS BUILT OF DRY BRANCHES, AND THE
PATH TO ITS ENTRANCE IS LINED WITH STONES
-ONE FOR EACH MAN THE DEAD CHIEF KILLED!

MEMBERS of the Rodiya Tribe, in Ceylon, BECAUSE AN ANCESTRESS NAMED PRINCESS VALLI BECAME A CANNIBAL, HAVE BEEN **OUTCASTS FOR 800 YEARS**

EVERY RODIYA WOMAN MUST USE THE NAME VALLI AND EACH MAN IS CALLED VILLIYA —AND NONE MAY EAT MORE THAN A SINGLE MEAL A DAY

THE **DEATH** OF A **COW** in Liechtenstein IS ALWAYS ANNOUNCED *BY AN OBITUARY IN THE LOCAL NEWSPAPER*

(Answer) HOW TO DISTRIBUTE THE DIGITS FROM 1 TO 9 IN THE SMALL CIRCLES SO THAT EACH LINE ADDS UP TO 15

ALEXANDER COCHRANE of Dundonald, Scotland, WAS THE FATHER OF **7 COLONELS** *ALL OF WHOM SERVED IN THE ARMY OF KING CHARLES I*

22

THE **10-DALER COPPER COIN** of Sweden *WORTH $7.20* WAS **27½** INCHES LONG, NEARLY A FOOT WIDE, AND WEIGHED **44** POUNDS

THE **IRON PAGODA OF HONAN,** China, BUILT **800** YEARS AGO IN THE BELIEF ITS WEIGHT WOULD HOLD DOWN THE GROUND -- *AND SO PREVENT EARTHQUACES!*

ALEXANDER **ADAM** (1741-1809) A HIGH SCHOOL TEACHER IN EDINBURGH, SCOTLAND, FOR **48** YEARS, COULD RECALL THE BIRTH DATE, MARKS AND OTHER PERTINENT FACTS ABOUT *EVERY STUDENT HE EVER TAUGHT*

CHING
Chief of the Chinese Beggars' Guild

RULED ALL CHINA AND ITS 400,000,000 PEOPLE FOR 3 YEARS!

FROM 1908 TO 1911 CH'ING ASSIGNED STREET CORNERS TO BEGGARS AND AT THE SAME TIME SERVED AS REGENT FOR HSUAN T'UNG-- WHO BECAME EMPEROR AT THE AGE OF 2½

SICKLES WERE ORIGINALLY MADE BY THE ANCIENT EGYPTIANS FROM *THE JAWBONES OF OXEN*

A WOODEN BAR
LINKING 2 TREES
in Zion, Va.,
HAS REMAINED
IN PLACE
SINCE 1790
-WHEN IT
SERVED AS AN
IMPROVISED
PULPIT
·FOR THE
COMMUNITY'S
FIRST
SERVICES

Dorothea Lynde DIX
1802-1889
OPENED A SCHOOL IN
WORCESTER, MASS., FOR THE
CHILDREN OF ITS ARISTOCRACY
*WHEN SHE HERSELF WAS
ONLY 14 YEARS OF AGE*

THE **GATE** TO A FARM IN
Boughton Monchelsea, England,
IS TOPPED BY A STONE SHAPED
LIKE A ROUND LOAF OF BREAD
-A WARNING TO MEDIEVAL
BAKERS AGAINST CHEATING
IN THE WEIGHT OF THEIR LOAVES

A **MOHAMMEDAN MOSQUE**

WITH A MINARET 225 FEET HIGH WAS CONSTRUCTED in Lednice, Czechoslovakia

—WHICH HAS NEVER HAD A MOHAMMEDAN RESIDENT—

PRINCE ALOIS LICHTENSTEIN ORDERED THE MOSQUE BUILT AT A COST OF $400,000 IN 1797

TO PUNISH THE TOWN FOR ITS FAILURE TO PROVIDE HIM WITH A SUITABLE SITE FOR A CHURCH

THE **CAPYBARA** IS THE LARGEST RODENT *IT WEIGHS 100 LB.*

THE RAINSPOUT ON A HOUSE on the Island of Helgoland, Germany,

WAS AN OLD LEATHER BOOT

A **CROCODILE** WHEN NEWLY HATCHED *IS 3 TIMES AS LARGE AS THE EGG FROM WHICH IT EMERGED*

SALLY MUTTON of Bristol, R.I., WAS PRONOUNCED DEAD IN 1900, BUT HER HUSBAND REFUSED TO ACCEPT THE DOCTOR'S STATEMENT -**AND HELD OFF THE UNDERTAKER WITH A SHOTGUN**

HE POURED HOT MILK BETWEEN HIS WIFE'S LIPS -AND SHE REGAINED CONSCIOUSNESS AND SURVIVED *HER HUSBAND BY 40 YEARS*

The "h" TREE
Submitted by
M.M. MIXSON,
Micanopy, Fla.

IN 8 HORSE RACES at Santa Anita Park, Arcadia, Calif., ALL RUN ON THE SAME DAY *EACH WAS WON BY A HORSE IN A DIFFERENT POST POSITION* (Feb. 6, 1963)

CHINESE BOXERS

FIGHT MATCHES IN WHICH THEY STRIKE BLOWS ONLY *WITH THEIR KNEES*

THE FIRST MAN TO LOSE HIS BALANCE FORFEITS THE CONTEST

THE DEVIL'S CHAIR
NATURAL FORMATION OF VOLCANIC GRANITE NEAR PUERTO NATALES, CHILE
Submitted by RICHARD FINNEY
Coral Gables, Fla.

AND I WAS GOING SWIMMING!

Worcester, N.Y., HAD 2 HEAVY SNOWFALLS ON JULY 18, 1876

QUEEN SQUARE in Bristol, England COVERS EXACTLY THE SAME AREA AS *THE GREAT PYRAMID OF EGYPT*

MAHARANI LAKSHMI BAI
FEMALE RULER of Jhansi, India, AND RINGLEADER OF THE GREAT INDIAN MUTINY OF 1857 AGAINST GREAT BRITAIN, *RODE 102 MILES ON HORSEBACK IN STEEL ARMOR -FIGHTING A RUNNING BATTLE ALL THE WAY* SHE WAS SLAIN AT THE END OF THE RIDE AND THE GREAT MUTINY ENDED

THE FIRST 20 MOVES IN CHESS CAN HAVE 169,518,829,100,544,000,000,000,000,000 VARIATIONS

THE MOSQUE of GHARDAIA
in Algeria
SERVES AS A LOST-AND-FOUND DEPARTMENT
VALUABLES FOUND IN THE COMMUNITY
ARE PLACED ON DISPLAY IN ITS WINDOWS
UNTIL THEY ARE CLAIMED BY
THEIR RIGHTFUL OWNERS

HARRY C. MACDONALD of Wilmington, Delaware, MADE A HOLE-IN-ONE AT THE Newark, C.C. —*WITH HIS BALL ENTERING THE CUP ON THE FLY*

Lawrence R. Dwight of Fortuna, Calif., CELEBRATED HIS FIRST BIRTHDAY *IN THE COMPANY OF 7 OF HIS GREAT-GRANDPARENTS*

A HUGE BOULDER SHAPED LIKE AN EGG AND WEIGHING 1,000 POUNDS WAS MOVED FROM YONKERS, N.Y., TO RIDGEFIELD, CONN., BY PAUL CORBALIS —AN INHERITANCE THAT HAS BEEN **PASSED DOWN IN HIS FAMILY FOR 5 GENERATIONS**

THE GREAT PAN ROAD up the Sacred Mountain of Tai Shan, China, HAS A SERIES OF HAIRPIN CURVES —**SO EVIL SPIRITS WILL HURTLE OVER THE PRECIPICES**

THE **FALTER TOWER** Kitzingen, Germany, **LEANS NEARLY 3 FEET FROM THE PERPENDICULAR**

KEITH M. HENRY
of Knoxville, Tenn.,
RODE
THE SAME MOTORCYCLE
FOR 50 YEARS

GRANDFATHER
*NATURAL
STONE PROFILE*
Grandfather Mountain, N.C.

THE **CHILEAN BEAVER**
IS THE ONLY MAMMAL IN NATURE THAT
FEEDS ITS OFFSPRING ON ITS BACK

Thomas TELFORD
(1757-1834) FAMED SCOTTISH ENGINEER, CONSTRUCTED 920 MILES OF ROADS AND **1,200 BRIDGES**

THE OLDEST STATUE IN THE WORLD

A CARVED HUMAN HEAD found buried near Lower Wisternitz, Czechoslovakia,

HAD BEEN CARVED FROM THE TUSK OF A MAMMOTH

IN THE ICE AGE 2,000,000 YEARS AGO

THE PUBLIC CLOCK in the Borghese Park, Rome, Italy, **IS RUN SOLELY ON WATER POWER**

A **MACKEREL**
PLACED IN A SMALL TANK
OF WATER **WILL DROWN**
*IT IS FORCED TO SWIM
SLOWLY AND ITS
GILLS CANNOT
SUPPLY ENOUGH
OXYGEN TO KEEP
THE FISH ALIVE*

A **BRIDE** in the Chaamba Tribe
of Southern Algeria
IS OFFICIALLY MARRIED
ONLY AFTER HER
HUSBAND HAS
SLAPPED HER 7 TIMES
*SHE MUST THANK HIM
FOR HIS ATTENTION AND
THIS IS THE FIRST AND
LAST TIME IN HER
LIFETIME SHE MAY CALL
HER HUSBAND BY NAME*

THE REV. CHARLES FRASER
of Elland, England,
WHILE A NAVAL CHAPLAIN
IN THE 19th CENTURY
PREACHED IN 7 COUNTRIES
*—ALWAYS IN THE
LANGUAGE OF THE AREA*
HE DELIVERED HIS SERMONS IN
ENGLISH, GREEK, HEBREW, LATIN,
ITALIAN, FRENCH AND SPANISH

SIR EDWARD CARSON WAS THE ONLY MAN IN HISTORY TO HOLD THE POST OF SOLICITOR GENERAL *IN BOTH ENGLAND AND IRELAND*

A **TALL PAGODA** in Tokyo, Japan, ORIGINALLY STOOD IN Seoul, Korea, AS THE JAPANESE EMPEROR'S WEDDING GIFT TO THE EMPEROR OF KOREA -BUT IN 1910 THE JAPANESE TOOK IT BACK

The MASHCOS of Peru
FAMED AS WARRIORS *LONG WORE THEIR MILITARY RANK* **ON THEIR FACES**

EACH TIME A MAN ADVANCED IN RANK ANOTHER LEAF WAS THRUST INTO HIS SKIN

THE **BELL** ATOP KORBACH HIGH SCHOOL, in Germany, INSTALLED THE DAY ON WHICH PROFESSORS KOENIG, WALDSCHMIDT AND WALDECK JOINED THE SCHOOL, CRACKED AND BECAME UNUSABLE 50 YEARS LATER *ON THE DAY THE 3 TEACHERS RETIRED* April 1, 1901

Dogs RIDING IN MOTOR CARS IN THE EARLY DAYS OF THE AUTOMOBILE *OFTEN WORE GOGGLES AND SPECIAL ATTIRE*

THE
**FIRST
MOUNTAIN
RAILROAD
IN THE U.S.**
So. Hadley, Mass.
A SINGLE-TRACK RAILROAD
RUNNING 600 FEET TO THE TOP
OF MOUNT HOLYOKE WAS BUILT IN 1851
WITH A CAR MADE FROM 2 SLEIGHS, WITH
A HORSE PROVIDING THE MOTIVE POWER

THE **HOLY WATER
BASIN**
in the Church
of St. Sulpice,
in Paris, France,
CONSISTS
OF 2 HUGE
SEA SHELLS
*ORIGINALLY
GIVEN TO
KING FRANCIS I
BY THE CITY OF
VENICE OVER*
400 YEARS AGO

POTATO TURTLE
Submitted by
MRS. THERESA SCOTT,
Gardena, Calif.

THE REV. HENRY DIXON
of Big Sandy Valley, Ky.,
AN ACCOMPLISHED VIOLINIST,
ALWAYS PLAYED THE FIDDLE
TO ENTERTAIN PARISHIONERS
*BEFORE AND AFTER
EACH SERVICE*

**CAPTAIN
THOMAS
WEST
PEYTON IV** of
Huntington, W.Va.,
WHO FOUGHT IN
WORLD WAR I

*WAS THE SON
OF CAPT. THOMAS
WEST PEYTON III
OF THE CIVIL WAR*

*THE GRANDSON
OF CAPT. THOMAS
PEYTON II OF THE
MEXICAN WAR*

*AND THE GREAT-
GRANDSON OF
CAPT. THOMAS WEST PEYTON
OF THE WAR OF 1812*

GLASS CATFISH
The Orient
ITS TRANSPARENT BODY REVEALS ITS SPINE AND BONES WITH ASTOUNDING CLARITY

THE **REV. JOHN LIVINGSTON**
(1603 - 1672)
ANCESTOR OF THE FAMED LIVINGSTON FAMILY OF AMERICA
WAS THE FIRST SCOTTISH MINISTER TO CARRY A WATCH

THE **MOSQUE** of **SANGAR el GAWLY** in Cairo, Egypt,
HAS NOT HAD A SINGLE WINDOW PANE BROKEN IN **659** YEARS

NATIVES HAVE CAREFULLY GUARDED ITS GLASS WINDOWS SINCE 1304 IN THE BELIEF A SINGLE CRACKED PANE WOULD RESULT IN **AN EGYPTIAN DISASTER**

PIONEER KENTUCKIANS IN THE YEARS JUST PRIOR TO 1800 TREATED WINTER COLDS BY SPENDING A NIGHT OUTDOORS IN THE DEEP SNOW BEFORE A ROARING FIRE—AND DRINKING *A PINT OF BEAR FAT*

ANDREW HALL (1722-1808) of Kinfauns, Scotland, AND HIS FATHER AND GRANDFATHER SERVED SUCCESSIVELY AS PARISH GRAVEDIGGERS *FOR A CONTINUOUS PERIOD OF 160 YEARS*

A HUGE HOLLOW IDOL

WAS BUILT OF WICKER BY THE DRUIDS OF ANCIENT GAUL AND BRITAIN ON CERTAIN HOLIDAYS AND FILLED WITH CRIMINALS —THEN SET ON FIRE!

THE FIRST MONEY

A COPPER INGOT MARKED "PURE" IN PHOENICIAN CHARACTERS WAS USED AS CURRENCY IN THE 16th CENTURY B.C.

RANNY SMETHERS of Othello, Wash., ON THE SECOND HOLE AT MOSES LAKE GOLF CLUB MADE A HOLE IN ONE HIS FATHER SCORED A BIRDIE 2 AND HIS BROTHER GREG HAD A PAR 3

STEPHAN LELAND
AN ENGLISHMAN LIVING
in Paris, France,
TO READ THE CHRONICLE
BY JEAN FROISSART
VISITED THE NATIONAL LIBRARY
DAILY FOR 29 YEARS
•ALWAYS TO READ THE SAME BOOK

THE **FRIENDLY EAGLE**
NATURAL STONE FORMATION
RESEMBLING AN EAGLE
IN THE ACT OF KISSING
A YOUNG GIRL
near Nish, Yugoslavia

**MEMORIAL
TO A
PUMP**

*"THIS OLD PUMP
NOW AT REST
STANDS AS A
MEMORIAL
TO THOSE IT
SERVED "*

PLAQUE ON A PUMP PRESERVED
IN CEMETERY AT OAK CREEK, WIS.
Submitted by Anne Monson,
South Milwaukee, Wis.

NATURE'S KNOT 2 *TREES* LINKED TOGETHER 10 FEET ABOVE THE GROUND

Submitted by ROLAND GILBERT Greenville, N.H.

JOHN MATTOCKS WHO WAS ELECTED GOVERNOR of Vermont in 1843 *NEVER MADE A CAMPAIGN SPEECH* HIS ONLY CAMPAIGN PROMISE WAS A PLEDGE TO HAVE **2 THANKSGIVINGS EACH YEAR**

WRIST WATCH THAT HAS KEPT PERFECT TIME —WITHOUT EVER BEING REPAIRED, CLEANED OR OILED— FOR **32 YEARS**

Owned by MISS CLAIRE SWEHLA Cedar Rapids, Iowa

THE MOSQUE OF SAMPGAON
Bombay
HAD **$25,000** IN GOLD SOVEREIGNS
IN PLAIN VIEW ON ITS ROOF
FOR **43** YEARS
*THE GOVERNOR OF SAMPGAON LEFT THE
GOLD THERE IN 1829 AND IT WAS FORGOTTEN
UNTIL HIS WILL WAS READ IN 1872*

THE GREEN FROG
(Phyllomedusa Yhering)
of Brazil
LAYS ITS EGGS ABOVE
A STREAM IN A
LEAF IT HAS ROLLED
INTO THE SHAPE
OF A FUNNEL
*SO THE HATCHED
TADPOLES CAN
SLIP DIRECTLY
INTO THE WATER*

NATIVES of the Ubangi Territory, in Africa,
ALWAYS MOVE THEIR VILLAGE AFTER A CHIEF'S DEATH,
TRANSPORTING EACH HUT ON 3 CANOES ACROSS A RIVER

THE BLUE FROG
(Phyllomedusa bicolor)
of Brazil

PROTECTS ITS
EYES FROM
MOSQUITO BITES
*BY ROLLING ITS
BULGING EYEBALLS
INSIDE ITS MOUTH*

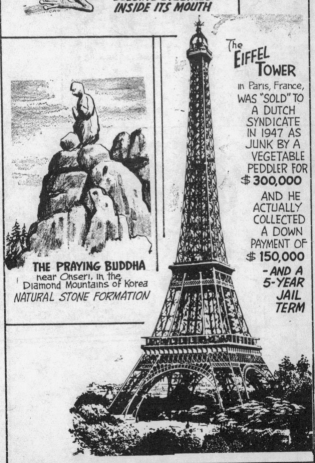

THE PRAYING BUDDHA
near Onseri, in the
Diamond Mountains of Korea
NATURAL STONE FORMATION

The
**EIFFEL
TOWER**
in Paris, France,
WAS "SOLD" TO
A DUTCH
SYNDICATE
IN 1947 AS
JUNK BY A
VEGETABLE
PEDDLER FOR
$300,000

AND HE
ACTUALLY
COLLECTED
A DOWN
PAYMENT OF
$150,000

– AND A
5-YEAR
JAIL
TERM

THE HEARTHSTONE
IN THE KITCHEN OF THE
BAY HORSE INN, Merrington, England,
ORIGINALLY WAS A
TOMBSTONE

THE **MAN** WHO HAD **10,000** TOMBSTONES!
KAN TANG
A CHINESE SCHOLAR
WHO SAVED HIS
EMPEROR FROM
ASSASSINATION
WAS SO REVERED FOR
HIS COURAGE THAT A
SPECIAL TOMBSTONE
ERECTED FOR HIM BY
THE GRATEFUL EMPEROR
*WAS DUPLICATED THROUGH-
OUT CHINA FOR 400 YEARS*

**KNEELING
ELEPHANT**
*NATURAL
STONE
FORMATION
IN PRILEP,
YUGOSLAVIA*
Submitted by
Stankovic Vladislav
Belgrade, Yugoslavia

THE MAGICIANS' BOOK

RECORDING THE SECRETS OF BATAK MAGICIANS of Indonesia

CONSISTS OF PAGES MADE FROM THE INNER BARK OF A TREE, AND THE INK, MADE FROM SOOT, *PERIODICALLY VANISHES*

LEWIS CROOKALL

of Blackpool, England, TO ATTEND A MEETING OF THE PRESTON GUILD, WALKED FROM BLACKPOOL TO PRESTON AND BACK — A DISTANCE OF **40 MILES** — *AT THE AGE OF 91*

THE CHAPEL of TRANSTAMARE

in the Cathedral of Cordoba, Spain, CANNOT BE ENTERED BECAUSE IT WAS BUILT HIGH UP ON ONE WALL OF THE CATHEDRAL *—AND NO STAIRWAY LEADS TO IT*

HANS WIESENJAGGL A POACHER of Kaltenbrunn, Austria, **ILLEGALLY KILLED 1,300 CHAMOIS** *-YET HE WAS PARDONED BECAUSE HE HAD PLEDGED TO HIS DYING FATHER THAT HE WOULD RETIRE* **AFTER BAGGING HIS 1,300th CHAMOIS**

WOMEN of Novi, Yugoslavia, STILL WEAR MOURNING FOR PETER ZRINY AND FRANZ FRANKOPAN *WHO WERE HANGED ON FALSE CHARGES OF TREASON* **294 YEARS AGO**

"KING TUT WAS MURDERED," SAYS J. CARTER BROWN, DIRECTOR OF THE NATIONAL GALLERY OF ART. BUT FURTHER INTRIGUE SURROUNDS TUT WHOSE BURIAL VAULT BEARS THE INSCRIPTION: *"DEATH WILL COME SWIFTLY TO THOSE WHO DISTURB THE CONTENTS!"* 12 PEOPLE WHO HELPED UNCOVER THE TOMB HAVE SINCE MET MYSTERIOUS DEATHS!

49

THE SHIP THAT SOUNDED ITS OWN DIRGE

THE "ATLANTIC", WRECKED OFF FISHER'S ISLAND, In Long Island Sound WAS POUNDED TO BITS ON THE ROCKY SHORE -YET ITS BELL CONTINUED TO FLOAT ON SUPPORTING TIMBERS **AND PEALED ON FOR DAYS** (1846)

THE FIRST TWO NAMES OF **ANNA EDE PASKERVILLE** READ THE SAME *FORWARD* AND BACKWARD Manchester, Iowa

CAPTAIN ETHAN CLARKE
(1745-1833)
MUSTERED OUT OF THE FIRST RHODE ISLAND REGIMENT AFTER THE AMERICAN REVOLUTION, *CONTINUED TO WEAR HIS UNIFORM DAILY* **FOR THE NEXT 50 YEARS**

THE SINGAPORE HOLLY

IS NOT FROM SINGAPORE -NOR IS IT A HOLLY *IT IS A NETTLE -AND FROM THE West Indies*

THE **GROUND MULLET**, THE **GULF KINGFISH** AND THE **SOUTHERN WHITING** ARE THE SAME FISH

DICK WILLIAMS of Scottsdale, Arizona, WON RINGS AND PARALLEL-BAR CHAMPIONSHIPS IN STATEWIDE COMPETITIONS -YET HIS LEFT LEG WAS CRIPPLED BY POLIO AND HAD TO BE KEPT STRAPPED TO HIS OTHER LEG

Children of the Madi Tribe, in Uganda, Africa, HAVING NEITHER CLASSROOMS NOR SLATES, USE THE OPEN DESERT AS THEIR SCHOOLHOUSE *AND WRITE THEIR LESSONS IN THE SAND*

51

CRAB ORCHARD STONE
A SANDSTONE QUARRIED in Cumberland County, Tenn.,
IS SO HARD THAT IT CAN CUT GLASS

HOMERO BLANCAS
of Houston University, Texas,
PLAYING ON THE PAR 70 PREMIER GOLF COURSE near Longview, Texas,
IN TOURNAMENT COMPETITION PLAYED THE LAST 18 HOLES IN ONLY 55 STROKES
HIS LAST 2 ROUNDS WERE 62-55 FOR 117
A WORLD'S RECORD FOR 36 HOLES
August 1962

THE **YELLOW BIRD'S NEST** a plant
GROWS WITHOUT SUNLIGHT AND IS UNABLE TO MANUFACTURE ITS OWN FOOD
—BUT ITS ROOTS ARE COVERED WITH A FUNGUS WHICH ENABLES IT TO EXTRACT NOURISHMENT FROM DECAYED LEAVES IN THE SOIL

THE **HUTS** BUILT BY SHEPHERDS
in Luberon, France,
CONSIST MERELY OF LOOSE
STONES WITHOUT MORTAR
-EXACTLY AS THEY WERE BUILT
IN THE SAME LOCALITY
THOUSANDS OF YEARS AGO

THE **LAZIEST** RULER IN HISTORY
GIAN GASTONE (1671-1737)
LAST MEMBER OF THE MEDICI FAMILY,
WAS IN PERFECT HEALTH,
YET HE GOVERNED FLORENCE, ITALY,
FOR 8 YEARS *FROM HIS BED*

THE SPRAY CARBURETOR

OF THE FIRST AMERICAN CAR WAS ADAPTED BY CHARLES DURYEA FROM HIS WIFE'S *PERFUME ATOMIZER* 1892

OPTICAL ILLUSION

IS IT A HEXAGON OR A CUBE?
Submitted by ROBERT TOWNSEND Rumford, Me.

THE CORPSE THAT RULED ETHIOPIA

EMPEROR MENELIK II
DIED ON SEPT. 10, 1911

BUT FOR 2 YEARS, 3 MONTHS AND 2 DAYS *HE WAS STILL CONSIDERED THE REIGNING MONARCH BY ALL HIS SUBJECTS*

THE MUSIC-LOVING BULL OF INGS

England
WHEN A RADIO BRINGS IT THE SOUND OF MUSIC *THE BULL STAMPS ITS FEET AND DANCES IN TIME WITH THE MUSIC*

THE **OFFICIAL SOBRIETY TEST** IN SOME RURAL COMMUNITIES in Italy REQUIRES THE SUSPECT TO PERFORM *A DANCE*

THE **SENTENCE** HANDED DOWN BY JUDGES IN 18th CENTURY CENTRAL EUROPE AGAINST A MEMBER OF THE COBBLERS' GUILD WAS IN THE FORM OF A DRAWING OF A COBBLER'S BENCH -WITH THE NUMBER OF BLOWS TO BE ADMINISTERED FOR EACH OFFENSE FORMING AN ADDITIONAL LEG TO THE BENCH

LEMON *SHAPED LIKE AN OCTOPUS* Submitted by CARL THOMPSON San Mateo, Calif.

SLOWE GOING and WAITE *WORK TOGETHER IN NEW YORK CITY*

THE FISH THAT CATCH THEMSELVES

MULLET ATTEMPTING TO RETURN TO THE MEDITERRANEAN WHEN THE SUMMER SUN HEATS THE WATERS OF LAKE BARDAWIL ARE CAUGHT IN HORIZONTAL NETS *INTO WHICH THE FRANTIC FISH LEAP BY THE HUNDREDS OF THOUSANDS* (Sinai Peninsula)

PRINCESS BREEZEWOOD R·A·PATSY A HOLSTEIN-FRIESIAN COW of Vienna, Ohio, *IN A PERIOD OF ONE YEAR PRODUCED* **1,866** POUNDS OF BUTTERFAT

CRICKET FIGHTS

STAGED BY THE CHINESE ARE ATTENDED BY HUGE CROWDS AND THE CONTENDERS ARE DIVIDED INTO CLASSES **—FIGHTING AS HEAVYWEIGHTS, MIDDLEWEIGHTS OR LIGHTWEIGHTS** *THE WINNER MUST CHIRP AFTER ITS VICTORY —OR IT IS DISQUALIFIED*

ADELAIDE HOCHE
(1776 - 1859)

WHOSE HUSBAND, FRENCH GENERAL LAZARE HOCHE, DIED IN 1799, REMAINED A WIDOW FOR 60 YEARS

HAVING REJECTED MARRIAGE PROPOSALS FROM 3 FRENCH FIELD MARSHALS - **ONE OF WHOM, BERNADOTTE, BECAME KING OF SWEDEN**

THE BLANKETS WORN BY NATIVES OF the Tonga Islands, in the South Pacific, ARE ADORNED BY A CRUDE DESIGN OF A PLANE - *A REMINDER THAT THE ISLANDERS CONTRIBUTED A SPITFIRE BEARING THEIR QUEEN'S NAME TO THE BRITISH IN WORLD WAR II*

A **BEER BARREL**

3½ FEET HIGH, SHAPED LIKE A BEER MUG, AND FORMERLY USED BY KINGS OF PRUSSIA, IS COMPLETELY COVERED WITH *HUNDREDS OF SILVER DOLLARS*

KING DHANA NANDA
of Magadha, India,

WAS ONE OF 8 BROTHERS WHO RULED THE COUNTRY SUCCESSIVELY FOR A PERIOD OF ONLY 12 YEARS

-EACH SUFFERING A VIOLENT DEATH !

(338 - 326 B.C.)

THE **WORM THAT WALKS LIKE A MAN**

Histriobdella A WORM THAT FEEDS ON LOBSTER EGGS *WALKS UPRIGHT ON 2 FLAT FEET*

AN **EXACT REPLICA OF THE GROTTO** of **LOURDES** in the Botanic Garden of Yanam, India, CONSTRUCTED BY AN AMERICAN ENGINEER IN 1944 WHEN HE RE-FLOATED A 1,000-TON SHIP AFTER A PRAYER -*ALTHOUGH IT HAD REMAINED FIRMLY WEDGED ON A ROCKY SHELF THROUGH A FULL YEAR OF LABOR*

THE LIE-DETECTOR BRIDGE

WITNESSES SUSPECTED OF LYING ON BALI WERE ORDERED TO CROSS A FRAIL BRIDGE TO THE TEMPLE OF BALI -*IN THE BELIEF THAT ONLY THE TRUTHFUL COULD NEGOTIATE THE FRAGILE SPAN*

A **PERSIAN CAT** OWNED BY THE ITALIAN DUKE OF *SPOLETO* WAS GIVEN THE ROYAL NAME OF TOMISLAW II *TO SHOW ITS OWNER'S DISAPPROVAL OF MUSSOLINI'S ACTION IN NAMING THE DUKE TO BE KING TOMISLAW II OF CROATIA*

THE **ELABORATELY CARVED DOORWAYS** in Mukalla, Arabia, ARE CONSIDERED SO IMPORTANT THAT THEY ARE USUALLY ERECTED FIRST – AND THEN A HOUSE IS **BUILT AROUND THEM**

THE **CECROPIA TREES** of So. America HAVE HOLLOW STEMS **WHICH SERVE AS NESTS FOR FEROCIOUS ANTS**

THE **LANTERN PUFFBALL** a fungus HAS OPENINGS THAT MAKE IT LOOK LIKE A PLASTIC PRACTICE GOLF BALL

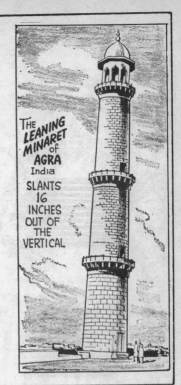

THE *LEANING MINARET* of **AGRA** India SLANTS 16 INCHES OUT OF THE VERTICAL

GEORGE WILLIAMS ANDREWES WAS MAYOR of Sudbury, England, in 1837 -THE YEAR QUEEN VICTORIA WAS CROWNED- AND SERVED IN THE SAME OFFICE **WHEN THE QUEEN CELEBRATED HER GOLDEN JUBILEE**

PADDY, THE RAM
A CHARACTER OF SYDNEY, AUSTRALIA,
IN SUMMER AND WINTER
*ALWAYS WORE 2 COATS, 4 SHIRTS
AND 3 PAIRS OF TROUSERS*

THE
REV. M.
HOYT
of Beadle
County, S.D.,
IN 55
YEARS
AS A
MINISTER
**BUILT
25
CHURCHES**

BUTTERNUT SQUASH

SHAPED LIKE
A SWAN

Grown by
ROBERT TREAT
Woodmont, Conn.

DUKE LOUIS de La TRÉMOILLE
(1838-1911) of France
DIED 120 YEARS AFTER THE DEATH OF HIS SISTER—
THE DUKE'S SISTER, CAROLINE, DIED AT THE AGE OF 2 —47 YEARS BEFORE THE BIRTH OF HER BROTHER

A MONUMENT TO BEEFSTEW
THE ORNATE MONUMENT in Carpentras, France, SHOWING A DISH COOKING OVER A BLAZING FIRE *COMMEMORATES POT-AU-FEU -- A TYPICAL FRENCH STEW*

A **CEMENT HOUSE** in Reynoldsville, Ill., *BUILT IN THE SHAPE OF AN ESKIMO IGLOO* Submitted by Richard Dembows, Detroit, Mich.

from an old print

THE WINE CASKS THAT WON A WAR!

DUKE ALEXANDER FARNESE CONQUERED ANTWERP, BELGIUM, BY FLOATING HIS ARTILLERY ACROSS THE RIVER SCHELDE *ON RAFTS SUPPORTED BY WINE BARRELS* (1585)

THE NEST of the MOSQUITO BEE of the Straits Settlements, Malaysia,

IS BUILT WITH A NARROW APPROACH PASSAGE

SO IT CAN BE MORE EASILY GUARDED AGAINST ATTACK

THE MOST ELABORATE BARN DOOR IN ALL BRITAIN
Newhall, England

A MAGNIFICENT DOORWAY WAS DESIGNED BY JAMES MOORE FOR A NEW HOME IN THE 17th CENTURY, BUT LITIGATION OVER THE PROPERTY USED UP ALL HIS FUNDS

—SO HE MADE IT THE ENTRANCE TO HIS BARN

THE LEDGERS THAT ARE ALWAYS OPEN FOR INSPECTION

NATIVES of New Guinea WEAR A BAMBOO NECK ORNAMENT

EACH STRIP OF WHICH REPRESENTS A PIG OR OTHER PIECE OF PROPERTY FOR WHICH SOMEONE OWES HIM PAYMENT

SERGIUS

A MONK in the monastery of Djebel el Tair, Egypt, BLESSED EVERY SHIP PASSING UP OR DOWN THE NILE BY SWIMMING TO THEM WITH HIS CLOTHING BALANCED ON HIS HEAD *-YET IN 31 YEARS HIS GARMENTS NEVER ONCE TOUCHED THE WATER!*

FISHERMEN
of the Cofan Tribe, in Colombia,
KILL THEIR CATCH BY
BITING EACH FISH'S NECK

THE **GREAT TEMPLE GATE**
of Shravanbelgola, India,
WAS CARVED FROM A
SINGLE BLOCK OF GRANITE

A *VIOLIN*
MADE
ENTIRELY FROM
**1,787
MATCHSTICKS**
*IT IS
PLAYABLE
AND HAS
A GOOD
TONE*

Submitted
by MRS.
DOLORES
WORTON
Dieterich, Ill.

SIR JOHN PRYCE (1698-1761)
of Newtown, Wales.
GRIEF STRICKEN BY THE DEATH
OF HIS WIFE, ELIZABETH,
*KEPT HER EMBALMED BODY IN THE
BEDROOM FOR 11 YEARS -EVEN AFTER HE HAD
TAKEN MARY MORRIS AS HIS 2nd WIFE*
WHEN MARY DIED HE HAD HER EMBALMED
BODY INSTALLED IN HIS BEDCHAMBER ALSO
·BUT HE DISPOSED OF BOTH BODIES AT
THE INSISTENCE OF HIS THIRD WIFE

A **COFFIN**, FOUND IN
Massarah, Egypt, in 1888
WAS MADE FROM THE ENTIRE
HIDE OF A CROCODILE

THE
**CALIFORNIAN
BLIND
GOBY**

LIVES IN CREVICES
IN ROCKS ON
THE SHORE

THE **KNEELING SATYR** in the Theatre of Dionysos, Greece, WAS GIVEN THE FACE OF SOCRATES BECAUSE ALCIBIADES, A PUPIL OF SOCRATES, 500 YEARS EARLIER SAID HIS MASTER RESEMBLED *"A DRUNKEN POT-BELLIED SATYR"*

THE **GRAND DUCHESS DETCHIN WANGMO** ruler of Kanze, Tibet, HAS BEEN DIVORCED *25 TIMES*

E.O. SAUNDERS of Pomeroy, Ohio, TAUGHT SCHOOL IN 3 STATES -OHIO, W.VIRGINIA AND KENTUCKY- *FOR A TOTAL OF 63 YEARS*

KING RADAMA II of Madagascar WAS ASSASSINATED WHEN HE ABOLISHED ALL POLICE FORCES AND RULED THAT ALL DISPUTES BETWEEN INDIVIDUALS AND MUNICIPALITIES MUST BE SETTLED *BY DUELS* (1863)

THE OLDEST HOUSE IN BRAZIL A DWELLING in Parahyba, Brazil, *USED CONTINUOUSLY FOR 365 YEARS*

A **GIANT SQUARE JELLYFISH**

WHICH DWELLS DEEP IN THE OCEAN

OFTEN IS THE NURSERY FOR **350** FISH

GENERAL AUGUSTE COLBERT
(1777-1809)

FIGHTING WITH NAPOLEON'S FORCES in the battle of Wagram, Austria, IN 1809, WAS HIT BY A BULLET THAT ENTERED NEAR HIS RIGHT EAR AND EMERGED THROUGH HIS LEFT EAR **-YET HE WAS NOT EVEN HOSPITALIZED!**

DOCTORS FOUND THAT THE BULLET HAD DETOURED INSIDE HIS SKULL AND HAD NOT DONE THE SLIGHTEST HARM

THE **SIGNATURE** OF MAURICE PHILIP the French poet WHOSE LAST NAME MEANS **"HORSE FANCIER"**

William FITZHARDING (1785-1857)
WAS MADE EARL of FITZHARDING AS A REWARD FOR HIS EFFORTS IN GETTING *ALL FOUR OF* HIS BROTHERS ELECTED TO THE BRITISH PARLIAMENT IN THE SAME YEAR (1841)

The **LEANING TOWER OF JIDDAH**

A MINARET in Saudi Arabia THAT IS TILTING *15 INCHES OUT OF LINE*

JAMES ISHERWOOD AN INNKEEPER IN Haslingden, England, TO WIN A WAGER

ATE 20 RAW EGGS IN 7 MINUTES -INCLUDING THEIR SHELLS

71

MRS. TWILA STEED
of Leachville, Ark.,
IS THE MOTHER
OF 4 SONS
*ALL BORN ON
OCT. 27th IN
DIFFERENT YEARS*

THE **WATCH TOWER**
of the
MEDIEVAL
FORTRESS OF
ST. MICHAEL,
on Malta
HAS A
HUMAN
EYE AND
EAR
CARVED
ON ITS
SIDES
-TO AID
IT IN
DETECTING
SURPRISE
ATTACKS

MRS. JOHN B. KIRBY
AND HER DAUGHTER,
MRS. MALCOLM KING,
members of the Pine
Orchard Y. and C.C.,
Branford, Conn.,
BOTH MADE HOLES-IN-
ONE ON THE SAME
HOLE DURING THE
SAME WEEK END
July 1963

GR-r-r-r

A **BULLDOG** owned by
Ludwig Hausing, manager of the
City Theatre, Glogau, Germany,
WAS NAMED "ADVANCE"
-AND TRAINED TO GROWL
OMINOUSLY WHEN ITS
NAME WAS MENTIONED
-TO DISCOURAGE ACTORS
FROM ASKING FOR AN
ADVANCE ON THEIR PAY

Here lyes the Body

Rob.t R.

Robt. RUSSAL
(1744-1771)
A STONE-CUTTER OF Newtownards, Ireland, CARVED HIS OWN EPITAPH ON A PILLAR IN THE LOCAL ABBEY WHEN HE WAS SEEMINGLY IN PERFECT HEALTH AND ONLY 27 YEARS OF AGE
-YET HE DIED OF NATURAL CAUSES AND WAS BURIED BESIDE THE PILLAR **ONLY A FEW DAYS LATER**

CUE VAS

COINS USED IN 18th CENTURY MEXICO WERE MINTED IN THE SHAPE OF LEAVES

THE BAPTISMAL FONT used for centuries in the Cathedral of Metz, France, WAS ORIGINALLY A BATHTUB *SALVAGED FROM AN ANCIENT ROMAN PUBLIC BATH*

73

Dr.
JULIUS TOWLER
(1811-1886)
of HOBART COLLEGE, Geneva, N.Y.,

SIMULTANEOUSLY TAUGHT

MATHEMATICS
PHILOSOPHY
CHEMISTRY
ANATOMY
PHYSIOLOGY
MODERN LANGUAGES
AND MEDICINE

OWLS HAVE BUILT IN "WINDSHIELD WIPERS"

THE **FOOTPRINTS** of the **MADONNA** WHERE THE MOTHER OF JESUS STOOD AS HE PASSED ON THE WAY TO CALVARY, ARE OUTLINED IN MOSAIC ON THE ROADWAY IN JERUSALEM

KILLOCHAN CASTLE in Girvan, Scotland, WAS GRANTED TO THE CATHCART FAMILY BY KING ROBERT BRUCE IN 1324, AND FOR NEARLY 500 YEARS ITS OCCUPANTS PAID TO THE ROYAL TREASURY AS AN ANNUAL RENTAL **3 SPEARS**

THE **BABACUT MONKEY** of Madagascar

AN ARDENT SUN BATHER

WILL SIT FOR HOURS IN THE SUN WITH HANDS OUTSPREAD AND ITS FACE UPTURNED

JOHN CRAGIN of Embden, Maine, WAS THE FATHER OF 5 DAUGHTERS *ALL OF WHOM BECAME SCHOOL-TEACHERS*

DR. W.M. MAC NEILL of Lillington, N.C., MARRIED A GIRL WHOSE BIRTH HE HAD ATTENDED **40 YEARS BEFORE**

THE **SAND HILL DWELLINGS** of the Amitermes termites of Panama ARE PALATIAL STRUCTURES

WHERE DO I VOTE?

NO MAN IN COLONIAL VIRGINIA WAS ENTITLED TO VOTE *UNLESS HE OWNED A CLOCK*

A **WILLOW TREE** in Baldwinsville, N.Y., GREW FROM THE RIDING CROP OF MRS. JONAS C. BALDWIN -WHICH SHE HAD STUCK INTO THE GROUND

THE ALASKAN BLACKFISH

IS SO HARDY IT SUFFERS NO HARM AFTER BEING *FROZEN SOLID IN ICE FOR A PERIOD OF WEEKS*

THE SOUND OF DOOM !

THE WHISTLE INSTALLED ON THE S.S. TELL CITY, at West Point, Ky., ALSO SERVED IN TURN THE S.S. EUGENE, THE PACKET HETTIE GILMORE, THE S.S. TARASCON AND THE PACKET SOUTHLAND *-EVERY ONE OF WHICH WAS DESTROYED BY FIRE OR SHIPWRECK*

ARAB WOMEN

MAY STOOP AT THEIR WORK *-BUT ARE FORBIDDEN TO KNEEL*

THE TAIL OF THE PORCUPINE

WAS USED BY THE CROW INDIANS AS A COMB

THE BONY BEARD OF THE WHALE

IS USED BY NATIVES OF FIRELAND, IN So. America *AS A HAIR COMB*

THE SVOBODNIKI

A RUSSIAN SECT of British Columbia

EAT NO MEAT, EGGS, FOWL OR DAIRY PRODUCTS, DRINK NO MILK, USE NEITHER LEATHER NOR WOOL AND DO ALL THEIR OWN WORK

IT IS AGAINST THEIR RELIGIOUS PRINCIPLES TO MAKE USE OF **ANY ANIMAL'S LABOR OR PRODUCT**

"THE POEM HOUSE"

near Stutzerbach, Germany, IS SO CALLED BECAUSE THE FAMED POET, GOETHE, WROTE *"The Night Song of the Wanderer"* **ON ONE OF THE BUILDING'S WOODEN WALLS**

THE REV. THOMAS M. ALLEN

of Paris, Ky., OFFERED THE NOMINATION FOR U.S. CONGRESS, DECLINED ON THE GROUNDS THAT IT WOULD *SET A BAD EXAMPLE FOR YOUNG MINISTERS*

AN ASSAULT TRIAL

WAS HELD IN THE COURT OF ASSIZES In Donegal, Ireland,

IN WHICH THE PLAINTIFF, THE DEFENDANT, THE PRESIDING JUSTICE, THE COURT CLERK, BOTH ATTORNEYS AND THE **3** WITNESSES *ALL WERE NAMED DOHERTY* (1835)

THE ISLAND THAT NEVER STANDS STILL!
MERCURY ISLAND
in the South Atlantic
IS SO HONEYCOMBED WITH TUNNELS
THAT THE POUNDING SEAS CAUSE IT TO
QUIVER LIKE QUICKSILVER!

A MICROCALORIMETER
INVENTED BY PROFESSOR E. CALVET
and used at the University of Montreal
CAN MEASURE THE TEMPERATURE OF A FLY'S BREATH

PUFFBALL THAT GROWS IN THE SHAPE OF A CROWN

THE BIG INDIAN
Amchitka Is., the Aleutians
NATURAL STONE FORMATION
Submitted by EMERY F. TOBIN, Ketchikan, Alaska

WILLIAM FRANCIS KING
(1807-1874) of Sydney, Australia,
WALKED 28 MILES IN 6 HOURS, 48 MINUTES, CARRYING A 104-LB. GOAT

THE AOUDAD OF North Africa IS BOTH A SHEEP AND A GOAT

DIONYSIUS
(431 B.C.–367 B.C.)
the tyrant of Syracuse

ALWAYS HAD HIS HAIR
AND BEARD TRIMMED
WITH RED-HOT COALS!

*HE WAS SO FEARFUL OF
ASSASSINATION THAT HE NEVER PERMITTED
A RAZOR OR SCISSORS NEAR HIS THROAT*

THE CANOES of the Sanapana Indians of the Gran Chaco, S.A., ARE MADE FROM THE TRUNKS OF THE BOTTLE TREE, THE WOOD OF WHICH IS SO SOFT IT CAN BE SCOOPED OUT WITH SPADES **–YET THE BARK IS AS HARD AS IRON**

THE
250,000
TURKISH SOLDIERS
WHO FOUGHT THE RUSSIANS
IN 1877 -WORE SILK SHIRTS
IN BATTLE IN THE BELIEF
THAT SINCE SILK DOES NOT
TEAR EASILY *A BULLET*
COULD BE EXTRACTED
FROM A WOUND MERELY
BY YANKING AT
THE SHIRT

THE
HIGHEST **LIGHTHOUSE**
IN THE WORLD
OLD POINT LOMA LIGHTHOUSE
in San Diego County, Calif.,
WHICH WAS OPERATED UNTIL 1891
IS 510 FEET ABOVE SEA LEVEL

THE
PALACE OF THE
TURKISH GOVERNOR
in Riadh,
capital of Saudi Arabia,
TO DEMONSTRATE THE
PRESENT GOVERNMENT'S
SCORN FOR THE TURKS,
WAS CONVERTED
INTO A PRISON

MRS. FRANCIS DE NICOLA of Weymouth, Mass., BECAME A MOTHER ON JULY 10, 1962 AT 5:53 P.M. AND GAVE BIRTH TO HER SECOND CHILD *EXACTLY ONE YEAR, ONE MONTH, ONE DAY AND ONE MINUTE LATER*

THE **REV. ROBERT QUARTERMAN** (1787-1849) of Midway, Ga., SAW HIS 4 SONS BECOME MINISTERS - AND MARRIED *HIS 2 DAUGHTERS TO MINISTERS*

THE **STARFISH FLOWER** (Stapelia gigantea) of South Africa LOOKS LIKE A STARFISH ENWRAPPED IN WEEDS

POLICE CHIEF **BYRON PARRISH** of Ranger, Texas, FAMED AS A PISTOL SHOT COULD THROW A CAN INTO THE AIR AND HIT IT 12 TIMES—FIRING SIMULTANEOUSLY WITH 2 SIX-SHOOTERS

THE **HAIRY FROG** of Africa IS COVERED WITH *FUR*

(Trichobatrachus robustus)

84

THE GENTLEMAN OF THE MOUNTAINS
NATURAL STONE FORMATION
Elkhorn Mountain,
Hardy County, W.Va.

The
PEAL
of
PEACE

LAKE VÄTTER— in Sweden
DEVELOPS HIGH WAVES
ON THE CALMEST DAYS
*WHENEVER WIND WHIPS UP
LAKE CONSTANCE, in Switzerland,
1,200 MILES AWAY*

THE BELL OF ROVERETO— *Italy*
WHICH IS RUNG TO OBSERVE
MEMORIAL DAYS THROUGHOUT
THE WORLD WAS CAST FROM THE
CANNON OF EVERY NATION THAT
FOUGHT IN WORLD WAR I
—BOTH FRIEND AND FOE

THE PROPHECY THAT TRICKED ITS VICTIM —

PRINCE JOZEF PONIATOWSKI
(1763-1813)
of Poland
AVOIDED BIRDS ALL HIS LIFE BECAUSE A GYPSY WARNED THAT HE WOULD BE **KILLED BY A MAGPIE**

THE PRINCE WAS DROWNED CROSSING GERMANY'S ELSTER RIVER

"ELSTER" IN GERMAN MEANS "MAGPIE"

THE CASTLE
of Bois de la Roche, in France,
WAS BUILT IN 1500 IN THE SHAPE OF A "V" *TO HONOR THE BUILDER'S DAUGHTER, VICTORINE*

THE MAN WHO RETURNED TO HAUNT THE COURT THAT TOOK HIS LIFE!

OSWALD KRÖL of Lindau, Germany, WAS CONVICTED OF MURDER AND EXECUTED! KRÖL WAS LATER VINDICATED —AND FOR 50 YEARS HIS SKELETON STOOD BEFORE THE JURIST WHO HAD PRONOUNCED THE DEATH SENTENCE!

GABES in the Tunisian Sahara, beside the Mediterranean, IS THE ONLY OASIS IN THE WORLD *LOCATED ON THE SEASHORE*

A **MONUMENT** ON A ROAD IN PERU BETWEEN LIMA AND CALLAO IS TOPPED BY A WRECKED AUTO *AND BEARS THE INSCRIPTION:* *"THE SLOWER YOU TRAVEL THE FURTHER YOU'LL JOURNEY"*

John **MCKEOWN** OF DIXIE, Idaho, *ALWAYS WORE 6 SUITS ONE OVER ANOTHER* **-AND CARRIED MONEY IN THE POCKETS OF EACH SUIT** HE DIED OF A COLD AFTER AUTHORITIES FORCED HIM TO TAKE HIS FIRST BATH

MRS. **RAY C. SCHOENHERR** OF Detroit, Mich., IS THE MOTHER OF 7 CHILDREN

JEANNETTE, BORN ON A **MONDAY**
KATHLEEN, BORN ON A **TUESDAY**
SUZANNE, BORN ON A **WEDNESDAY**
ANDREW, BORN ON A **THURSDAY**
THOMAS, BORN ON A **FRIDAY**
MARY, BORN ON A **SATURDAY**
JOSEPH, BORN ON A **SUNDAY**

COUNT ALEXIS BESTUZHEV-RIUMIN
(1695-1766) of Russia
A DIPLOMAT FOR HALF A CENTURY,
ROSE TO BECOME CHANCELLOR
OF THE RUSSIAN EMPIRE
*BECAUSE HE MUMBLED SO BADLY
HE COULD ALWAYS CLAIM HE
HAD BEEN MISUNDERSTOOD*

HANDMADE ALMANACS
WERE WORN
SUSPENDED FROM
A CHAIN BY
14th CENTURY
ENGLISH
HOUSEWIVES AS
*A REMINDER
OF WHEN TO
PERFORM*
DOMESTIC CHORES

THE **CAPERCAILLE**
CAN ONLY BE CAUGHT
WHILE IT GOBBLES

MELCHIOR KHLESL
(1552-1630)
of Vienna, Austria,

WHO FELT PRAYER HAD CURED HIM OF LEPROSY *PRAYED IN THE SAME CHURCH EVERY DAY THEREAFTER FOR 53 YEARS*

THE HOUSE THAT COMPRISES AN ENTIRE VILLAGE
TAGADIRT
in the Atlas Mountains of Morocco
HAS A POPULATION OF 1,001 PERSONS
-ALL OF WHOM LIVE IN A SINGLE TERRACED STRUCTURE

THE HUMAN PINCUSHION

CAPT. LEWIS KRAATZ (1773-1858) of Independence, Texas, WAS LEFT FOR DEAD ON THE PRAIRIE BY INDIANS —WITH 27 ARROWS IN HIS BODY— *HE RECOVERED AND LIVED ANOTHER 18 YEARS*

THE **"WEDDING RING"** OF ARAMIA TRIBESMEN, OF NEW GUINEA, IS A **CONICAL CAP DONNED ON THEIR WEDDING DAY.** *THE HAIR GROWS THROUGH THE MESH AND MAKES IT IMPOSSIBLE TO REMOVE THE CAP*

JACOB BURVIN FUNKHOUSER
of Hambleton, W.Va.,
TO PAY OFF AN ELECTION BET
IN 1936 CRAWLED FROM HAMBLETON
TO PARSONS, A DISTANCE OF 2 MILES,
IN 3½ HOURS – *ALTHOUGH HE
WAS 60 YEARS OF AGE*

BIRD IN ITS BATH
NATURAL ROCK FORMATION
in the Enchanted Valley, Argentina

**WILLIAM
MARGRAVE**
of Fort Scott,
Kansas,
SIMULTANEOUSLY
SERVED AS
*JUSTICE OF
THE PEACE
CLERK OF
THE COURT
PROBATE
JUDGE*
AND *POLICE
JUSTICE*

RABBITS CAN RUN FASTER *UPHILL THAN DOWN*

THE **DUKE** OF **CAXIAS** (1803-1880) FAMED SOLDIER AND STATESMAN *WAS THE ONLY BRAZILIAN DUKE IN THE COUNTRY'S HISTORY*

OSKAR FRANZ (1885-1956) CARRYING **44** POUNDS OF BRICKS IN A PACK CLIMBED MT. HOCHSCHWAB, in Austria, TO ITS 7,500-FOOT-HIGH PEAK *297 TIMES - JUST FOR EXERCISE*

93

KARL DEWEY MYERS (1899-1951)
who became Poet Laureate
of West Virginia
WAS A CRIPPLE WHO NEVER WEIGHED
MORE THAN 60 POUNDS AND
WAS COMPLETELY SELF-EDUCATED

*HE MEMORIZED THE DECLARATION
OF INDEPENDENCE, THE CONSTITUTION
OF THE U.S., THE MAYFLOWER COMPACT
AND THE MAGNA CHARTA*

THE **STRANGEST
CHRISTMAS
SHOPPING IN
THE WORLD**

THE **NIGHT** OF
RADISHES

A MARKET
SET UP IN
Oaxaca,
Mexico,
EACH
CHRISTMAS
EVE
SELLS ONLY
RADISHES
-BUT EACH
ONE IS
MADE TO
LOOK LIKE
A PERSON
OR ANIMAL

THE LLOG
A CROSS BETWEEN
A LLAMA AND A DOG

The **NEST** OF THE MASON BEE IS CONSTRUCTED INSIDE THE WHORLS OF *AN ABANDONED SNAIL SHELL*

SANTA CLAUS

AS THE FAT, JOLLY, RED-CHEEKED, WHITE-WHISKERED, UNIVERSALLY RECOGNIZED ST. NICK, WAS CREATED BY CARTOONIST THOMAS NAST *OVER 100 YEARS AGO!*

A **PORTABLE** SUN DIAL USED IN 18th CENTURY ENGLAND, WAS SHAPED LIKE A NAPKIN RING

—A RAY OF LIGHT PASSING THROUGH AN APERTURE TO ILLUMINATE MARKINGS INSIDE THE RING

THE OLD TOLL BRIDGE between New York and City Island
WAS BUILT IN 1873 WITH TIMBER SALVAGED FROM
THE 90-GUN BATTLESHIP NORTH CAROLINA

THE
CONUS SNAIL
of the South Pacific
IS SO POISONOUS
THAT ITS BITE
CAN KILL A MAN

KING WENZEL (1361-1419)
of Germany
WAS SO POVERTY STRICKEN
THAT TO FEED HIMSELF AND
HIS COURT HE OFTEN
HOCKED HIS CROWN

A DUGOUT CANOE
IN USE CONSTANTLY ON
Lake Walchen, Bavaria,
FOR 210 YEARS

THE **NEST** of
Brazilian wasps
IS A CARDBOARD
DRUM *MANUFACTURED*
BY THE WASPS
FROM WOODPULP

THE **MAN** WHOSE LIFE BEGAN AND
ENDED IN THE SAME PRISON CELL
ANTONIO BIANCANI (1699-1746)
A BANKER OF MILAN, Italy,
WAS BORN IN A CELL IN THE
STATE PRISON, AND 47 YEARS
LATER, AFTER HIS CONVICTION
FOR HIGH TREASON
WENT TO HIS DEATH
FROM THE SAME CELL

THE **NEST** OF THE GREAT SILVER WATER BEETLE IS BUILT OUT OF 2 CONCAVE LEAVES *AND EQUIPPED WITH A SNORKEL* -TO SUPPLY AIR TO THE BEETLE'S LARVA

McKINLEY ROCK
A STONE PROFILE NEAR Thurmond, W.Va, WAS CREATED WHILE BLASTING FOR A RAILROAD ON Sept. 6, 1901 -*THE DAY ON WHICH PRESIDENT McKINLEY WAS FATALLY SHOT BY AN ASSASSIN*

NANCY JANE CLARK
(1844-1947) of Farmington, Kentucky, SAW 9 OF HER GREAT-GRANDSONS GO OVERSEAS TO FIGHT *IN WORLD WAR II*

98

THE TOWN of DUIRAT
in Southern Tunisia
IS ENTIRELY LOCATED
INSIDE A SINGLE MOUNTAIN

A SIEGE TOWER

CONSTRUCTED FOR JULIUS CAESAR
BY GENERAL TREBONIUS OUTSIDE
THE WALLED CITY OF MARSEILLES

WAS STARTED BY BUILDING A
ROOF OF ANIMAL FUR AND ROPE
TO PROTECT THE WORKMEN
AGAINST THE DEFENDERS' ARROWS
- AND THEN THE ROOF WAS
RAISED HIGHER AND HIGHER
TO A HEIGHT OF 6 STORIES

THE LEAPING SHELL
THE AUSTRALIAN TRIGONIA,
a type of mollusk,
CAN LEAP 14 INCHES

A CHRISTMAS TREE
ERECTED FOR A HOLIDAY
CELEBRATION BY STUDENTS
at Kansas State University
*WAS MADE FROM 2
HUGE TUMBLEWEEDS*

DAVID POLK
A LETTER CARRIER
of Montrose, Scotland,
TO SAVE THE SOLES
OF HIS BOOTS ALWAYS
WALKED ON TIPTOE

THE **GREAT CASTLE of HIROSAKI**
in Japan
HAS STOOD FOR MORE THAN 300 YEARS
- YET ITS FOUNDATION CONSISTS
ONLY OF A PILE OF LOOSE
STONES WITHOUT MORTAR

THE CHATEAU THAT ACTUALLY WAS SOLD FOR PEANUTS

BONAGUIL CASTLE
France

WAS BOUGHT IN 1800
BY JEAN LA GRAVE
FOR 41 BAGS OF PEANUTS!

YAKCOWS of Mongolia
OFFSPRING OF A YAK AND A COW

THE LEAF BUG of So. America
AS A DISGUISE AGAINST ITS ENEMIES HAS
HIND LEGS WITH "CALVES" SHAPED LIKE LEAVES

GUATEMALA
HAS ITS HIGHLANDS SEPARATED
FROM ITS LOWLANDS BY
*A CHAIN OF 32
ACTIVE VOLCANOES*

THE **CHORTEN**
OF **TASSIDING, India,**
IS CONSIDERED SO SACRED
*THAT THE MERE SIGHT OF IT
CLEANSES A MAN OF ALL SIN*

A **MONKEY**
OWNED
BY BRITISH
EXPLORER
RICHARD
BURTON
(1821-1890)
*WORE
EARRINGS
WITH REAL
ORIENTAL
PEARLS*

The PAGODA of PAIT'ATZE in Mongolia WHICH IS 325 FEET HIGH STILL STANDS AND ITS 680 BELLS STILL RING -YET EVERY OTHER STRUCTURE IN THE 900-YEAR-OLD CITY WAS DESTROYED BY A STORM

THE ELECTRIC CHAIR PLANT (Dionea muscipula) ELECTROCUTES ITS INSECT VICTIMS

Mrs. Kate A. GOULD of Glencoe, Minn., STILL WORKED AS CASHIER IN THE BOX OFFICE OF A MOVIE THEATRE AT THE AGE OF 93

A **COAL MINE**
near Neunkirchen, Saar, Germany,
LOCATED ABOVE THE GROUND

THE LAUGH THAT SAVED A LIFE!
LORD NORBURY
(1745-1831)
Chief Justice of Ireland,
GIVEN ONLY A FEW HOURS TO LIVE
SENT WORD TO A DYING FRIEND
"IT WILL BE A DEAD HEAT
BETWEEN US!"
*HIS OWN JEST CAUSED LORD NORBURY
TO LAUGH UPROARIOUSLY
AND DOCTORS CREDITED THE JOKE
WITH SAVING HIS LIFE*

THE V FALLS
of Leura, New So. Wales
-FORMED BY THE CONVERGING OF
2 GREAT STREAMS OF WATER

104

THE **DOORWAY** TO **HAPPINESS**

THE GATEWAY of the PAGODA of URGA, Mongolia, WAS USED BY EVERY MONGOLIAN ABOUT TO START ON A JOURNEY, FOR A PERIOD OF 1,000 YEARS

-IN THE BELIEF IT ASSURED TRAVELERS A JOYFUL TRIP

ROGER ZUBARIK
of Goldsboro, N.C.,
PLAYING FOOTBALL WITH THE Little League Green Bay Packers

SCORED 2 TOUCHDOWNS IN THE FIRST 26 SECONDS OF A GAME (Dec. 8, 1962)

THE **HORN** OF **PLENTY**

A SHELL FOUND IN THE FAR EAST

IS USED AS A CANDY CONTAINER

THE **LEAF** OF THE UMBRELLA TREE
IS SHAPED LIKE A ROUND FAN

Dr. Thomas SPENCER
(1679-1754)

THE FIRST WHITE CHILD BORN
In East Greenwich, R.I.,
NEVER STUDIED MEDICINE, BUT WAS
ACCREDITED AS THE COMMUNITY'S
FIRST PHYSICIAN —*MERELY*
BECAUSE HE WAS HIS
PARENTS' 7th SON—
HE WAS A DOCTOR FOR
MORE THAN 50 YEARS

GENERAL GEORGE H. WARD
(1826-1863) of Worcester, Mass.,
WHO LOST A LEG IN THE BATTLE OF
BALLS BLUFF, WAS KILLED AT GETTYSBURG
WHILE LEADING HIS TROOPS
ON A WOODEN LEG AND A CRUTCH
July 3, 1863

CLOCK MADE FOR
KING CHARLES II
FROM A
HUMAN SKULL

EDMUND WISEMAN
(1562-1644)
WHOSE FAILURE TO DELIVER A PLEA OF CLEMENCY TO QUEEN ELIZABETH I WAS RESPONSIBLE FOR THE DEATH OF THE EARL OF ESSEX

VOWED HE WOULD NEVER AGAIN SLEEP IN A BED

HE SLUMBERED IN A TREE WITHOUT BEDDING EVERY NIGHT FOR 43 YEARS

-UNTIL HIS DEATH AT THE AGE OF 82

THE **DEVIL'S TABLE**
Viechtach, Germany
NATURAL STONE FORMATION

MOSQUITOES
PREFER BLONDES—A BRUNETTE'S SKIN OFFERS MORE RESISTANCE

A RACE HORSE in England WAS NAMED:

"CRYTOCHONCHOPAYASTIGMATIC"

KING KUMARA DASA

who ruled Ceylon from 515 to 524
WAS SO FERVENT AN ADMIRER OF
THE WORKS OF HIS COURT
POET, KALIDASA, THAT HE
*KILLED HIMSELF BY
LEAPING ONTO THE POET'S
FUNERAL PYRE*

JOSÉ LUIS
of La Roda, Spain,

— WAS STRICKEN WITH
PNEUMONIA **32** TIMES
*-AND EACH TIME RECOVERED
WITHOUT THE USE OF PENICILLIN*

THE GUARDIAN OF THE NOTCH
A HUNTER AND
HIS DOG
*NATURAL STONE
FORMATION*
Smugglers Notch,
Cambridge, Vt.

BAMBOO MONEY

USED IN THE 19th CENTURY BY *THE CHINESE*

EPIPHYTIC ORCHIDS —

GROW IN THE BRANCHES OF HIGH TREES AND **EACH HAS 3 TYPES OF ROOTS**

ONE TYPE OF ROOT SUPPORTS THE ORCHID BY TWINING AROUND BRANCHES, ANOTHER DROPS TO THE GROUND TO DRAW NOURISHMENT FROM THE SOIL, AND THE THIRD TYPE ABSORBS MOISTURE FROM THE AIR

KING EDWARD IV
(1442-1482) of England

WAS THE FIRST ROYAL FISHERMAN IN HISTORY

KING EDWARD, WHO ADOPTED THE SPORT FORMERLY ENGAGED IN ONLY BY HIS MOST HUMBLE SUBJECTS, CAUGHT A FATAL COLD WHILE FISHING

A **COIN**

MINTED IN Korea in 1464 WAS SHAPED LIKE AN ARROWHEAD *4 INCHES IN LENGTH*

THE **MEMORIAL** in Dartmouth, England, TO THE DEAD OF WORLD WARS I AND II *ORIGINALLY SERVED AS A BAPTISMAL FONT* **300 YEARS AGO**

DROPS OF BLOOD FROM THE FINGER OF MACHINIST MATTHEW MATHIS, BLOTTED UP BY A PIECE OF COPY PAPER, FORMED A PERFECT PICTURE *OF A FRENCH POODLE*

Submitted by DOROTHY HAMILL Johnson City, Tenn.

JAMES FLETCHER of Terryville, Conn., IS THE WINNER OF **11** MEDALS AND **13** TROPHIES FOR ROLLER SKATING, AND WAS *THE* MEN'S FIGURE-SKATING CHAMPION OF CONNECTICUT. *—YET HE HAS A PARALYZED LEG, AND SKATES WITH METAL BRACES*

CAVE FISH of Mexico ARE SIGHTLESS—YET THEY HAVE SUCH SENSITIVE "RADAR" *THEY NEVER COLLIDE WITH ANYTHING*

JOHN ERICSSON
(1803-1889)
The famed naval engineer

WAS OFFICIAL DRAFTSMAN OF THE SWEDISH CANAL COMPANY **AT THE AGE OF 12**

HE HEADED A LABOR FORCE OF 400 MEN IN THE CONSTRUCTION OF SWEDEN'S GÖTA CANAL WHEN **HE WAS ONLY 14**

THE **FIRST TOOL**

A STONE AXE found at St. Acheul, France WAS CARVED BEFORE THE AGE OF MAN *1,000,000 YEARS AGO*

THE **OLDEST TAVERN IN THE U.S.**
THE WHITE HOUSE TAVERN in Newport, R.I.,
HAS BEEN OPERATING FOR 291 YEARS

4 AUSTRIAN OFFICIALS

WHO REGULARLY ROWED TOGETHER EACH SUNDAY ON THE DANUBE

WERE ORDERED DROWNED BY PRINCE von KAUNITZ, CHANCELLOR OF AUSTRIA,

BECAUSE HE HAD LEARNED ONE OF THEM WAS A SPY FOR PRUSSIA **—YET THE PRINCE KNEW THE OTHER 3 MEN WERE INNOCENT**

PENNIES in British West Africa in 1936 WERE MADE OF **NICKEL**

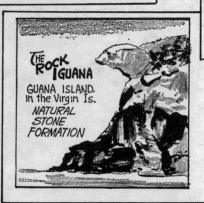

THE ROCK IGUANA

GUANA ISLAND, in the Virgin Is. *NATURAL STONE FORMATION*

THE **HUGE** **THRONE** OF King Mpande of the Zulus WAS CARVED FROM A *SINGLE BLOCK OF WOOD*

NATIVES of the Quiquijana Tribe of Cuzco, Peru, IN A DANCE IMPERSONATING A STORM-TOSSED SHIP—*MUST* *BALANCE A MAST 20 FEET HIGH*

STONE HEAD Submitted by ERIC LEVY Revere, Mass.

THE **DWELLINGS**
OF THE DOGON NATIVES
of Macina Province, West Africa,
CONSIST ENTIRELY OF ROCKS
PILED ONE ATOP ANOTHER
WITHOUT THE USE OF MORTAR.

NATIVES
of Noumea
island in
the Pacific

SHOOT
FISH WITH
A BOW
-USING
AS THEIR
ARROW AN
8-FOOT
SPEAR

*THEY FEEL
THAT THEIR
WEAPON
GIVES THEM
SUCH AN
ADVANTAGE
THEY SHOOT
ONLY AT
EVERY 3d
FISH THEY
SEE*

IF A YOUNG TWIN DIES IN THE YORUBA TRIBE of Nigeria, Africa, THE SURVIVOR MUST CARRY AROUND A WOODEN STATUE OF THE DEAD TWIN --WHICH IS CLOTHED LIKE THE SURVIVING TWIN EVERY DAY AND GIVEN THE SAME FOOD

THE TEMPLE ON THE THRONE OF SOLOMON a mountain near Srinagar, Kashmir, WAS BUILT IN 220 B.C. OF LOOSE STONES WITHOUT MORTAR --YET IT HAS ENDURED FOR NEARLY 22 CENTURIES

THE CITY of DUNFERMLINE in Scotland

WAS LEASED TO QUEEN ANNE BY HER HUSBAND, KING JAMES VI, **FOR THE ANNUAL RENTAL OF ONE PENNY**

THE PENNY WAS PAYABLE EACH YEAR ON THE 7th SUNDAY AFTER EASTER — AND IF THE QUEEN HAD FAILED TO MAKE A SINGLE PAYMENT ON TIME THE CITY WOULD HAVE REVERTED TO THE KING

SHE WAS
TWICE 6
TWICE 7
TWICE 20
AND 11

INSCRIPTION ON TOMBSTONE
Churchyard of
Wistanstow,
England

DR. CHARLES STEINMETZ
the electrical wizard
NEVER LEARNED TO OPERATE A CAR
BECAUSE HE HIT A TREE ON HIS FIRST ATTEMPT TO DRIVE

A **BAR GATE**
LAID ON THE GROUND
HORIZONTALLY IS USED ON
MANY CANADIAN RANCHES
*BECAUSE CATTLE WILL NEVER
WALK THROUGH SUCH A GATE*

**MOHAMMED
IQBAL** (1876-1938)
AN INDIAN POET
IN HIS EPIC POEMS
*FIRST SUGGESTED THE CREATION
OF THE INDEPENDENT MOHAMMEDAN
STATE OF PAKISTAN*

General Postage
NOT
EXCEEDING
HALF
AN OUNCE
One Penny.

A **POSTAGE STAMP**
WAS SUGGESTED
TO THE BRITISH
GOVERNMENT BY
JAMES CHALMERS,
of Dundee, in 1834
*—6 YEARS
BEFORE
OFFICIAL
INVENTION
OF THE
POSTAGE
STAMP BY
ROWLAND
HILL*

COLOGNE, Germany,
FOR DEMOLISHING ITS
700-YEAR-OLD CITY WALLS
WITHOUT FIRST GETTING
APPROVAL OF THE PRUSSIAN
GOVERNMENT, WAS ORDERED
TO WEIGH THE DEBRIS AND
PAY THE GOVERNMENT
*ITS "ASSESSED VALUE"
OF $3,000,000* (1881)

THE
**FAT-
RUMPED
SHEEP** of Asia and Africa
ARE PROTECTED AGAINST
PERIODS OF FAMINE
*BY A LAYER OF FAT
STORED ON THEIR BACKS*

THE **TOMBS** of Haitian peasants
ARE OFTEN RESPLENDENT STRUCTURES
*EVEN THOUGH THEY MAY HAVE LIVED
ALL THEIR LIVES IN WRETCHED HUTS*

THE MARBLE STATUE
of Lady Jane Cheyne
in Chelsea Old Church, London, England,

WAS BLOWN THROUGH A SOLID STONE WALL BY A NAZI BOMB IN WORLD WAR II AND BURIED IN THE RUBBLE OF THE CHURCH
-YET IT WAS FOUND UNDAMAGED EXCEPT FOR MINOR SCRATCHES

THE **TOMB OF CYRUS THE GREAT**
FOUNDER OF THE PERSIAN EMPIRE
located in Pasargadae, Iran,
HAS BEEN THE RESIDENCE OF A SUCCESSION OF FORTUNE TELLERS
FOR 2,000 YEARS

THE **GOBLIN** of Narvik, Norway

NATURAL STONE FORMATION

School Children
in Chad, Africa,
TO SHOW THEIR RESPECT
*TURN THEIR BACKS
TO THEIR TEACHERS*

A GREAT WINDOW
in the Manor of Leybourne, England,
SERVES AS A SUN DIAL

DUCK
CROSSING
SLOW

SIGN IN
WEST FALMOUTH, MASS.

A **HUGE BOULDER** near Arequipa, Peru, **SPLIT OPEN BY A CACTUS**

A **WOMAN** of the Motilones Tribe of Colombia DANCING IN TRIBAL FESTIVITIES MUST CARRY ON HER BACK *A BAG FILLED WITH THE BONES OF DECEASED RELATIVES*

THE STABLES BUILT IN SAAS-FEE, Switzerland, ARE ALWAYS REPLICAS OF THE DWELLINGS CONSTRUCTED BY THE TOWN'S ANCESTORS *IN ANCIENT TIMES*

LONGLEAT HOUSE
in England
WAS RENOVATED IN 1808 BY
THE 2d MARQUESS OF BATH
WHO RAISED THE FUNDS BY
COLLECTING FROM EACH
TENANT ON HIS ESTATE
20 YEARS' RENT IN ADVANCE

RALPH SIEDEL
of Strongsville, Ohio,
A GRADUATE OF
WILMINGTON COLLEGE,
WORE A CAP AND
GOWN PURCHASED BY
HIS FAMILY IN 1927
**AND WORN BY 28
MEMBERS OF THE
FAMILY AND FRIENDS**

THE OLDEST WIG IN THE WORLD
IT WAS FOUND IN
THE GRAVE OF
EGYPTIAN PRINCESS
ENTIU-NY AND
WAS INTERRED
WITH HER IN
1049 B.C.
**-MORE THAN
3,000
YEARS AGO**

Timothy McCARY of Birmingham, Alabama, AT ONE YEAR OF AGE HAD 13 LIVING GRANDPARENTS

THE COWBOY BAND of Dodge City, Kansas, WAS LED FROM 1881 TO 1887 BY A BANDLEADER WHO USED AS HIS BATON A LOADED SIX-SHOOTER

PROFILE ROCK near Gehlberg, Germany, ACTUALLY HAS 2 PROFILES CARVED BY NATURE — ON ONE SIDE THAT OF A MAN, AND ON THE OTHER THE HEAD OF A DOG

LEMON
SHAPED LIKE THE HEAD OF A WITCH
found by Susie and Donna Hardwick Los Angeles, Calif.

The **STATUES** that **CHANGED THEIR COIFFURES**

EMPRESS ANNA LUCILLA (147-183) of Rome

HAD A NUMBER OF WIGS OF VARIOUS HUES

—SO EVERY STATUE OF THE EMPRESS WAS CREATED WITH **INTERCHANGEABLE MARBLE HAIRDOS**

PUMPKINS, GROWING IN Um Ramad, Sudan, **ON THE THATCHED ROOF OF A HOUSE**

A PUBLIC LIBRARY WAS ESTABLISHED IN Chicago, Illinois, in 1871 *IN AN ABANDONED WATER TANK*

A TOMATO PLANT GROWING OUT OF A CONCRETE YARD in Sydney, Australia, HAS REACHED A HEIGHT OF 19 FEET - *AND IS STILL GROWING*

Submitted by Edward O'Sullivan Fairfield. New So. Wales

GENERAL NORD-ALEXIS (1820-1910) STARTED THE REVOLUTION WHICH OVERTHREW THE GOVERNMENT OF HAITI IN 1902 *WHEN HE WAS 82 YEARS OF AGE*

125

A CASH REGISTER
USED EVERY WEEKDAY **FOR 53 YEARS**

Submitted by
Allen Munro
Malden, Mass.

HENRY CAREY
OVER A PERIOD OF 80 YEARS
WAS VALET TO 6 BRITISH RULERS
HE SERVED JAMES I, CHARLES I, OLIVER CROMWELL, CHARLES II, JAMES II AND WILLIAM III
(1615 - 1695)

Gladiolus
WITH **4** FLOWERING STEMS

Submitted by
MRS. ALICE FEILING
Kentfield, Calif.

ANTS TO CROSS FROM ONE LEAF TO ANOTHER **FORM A LIVING BRIDGE**

126

YOUNG LAMBS
BECAUSE OF A SHORTAGE OF SHEEP DOGS In Syria ARE TRAINED TO GUARD THE FLOCKS

THE STONE CAMEL
NATURAL FORMATION
Luray Caverns, Virginia

ANDREW MILLS of Spennymoor, England, HANGED AND PLACED IN A CAGE FOR THE MURDER OF 3 CHILDREN, REMAINED ALIVE ON THE SCAFFOLD FOR SEVERAL DAYS

THE **COEDARHYDYGLYN HOUSE**
atop Tumble Hill, in Glamorgan, Wales,
OVERLOOKS 7 COUNTIES
IN WALES AND ENGLAND

THE FLOWER THAT "WALKS"
NEOMATICA GRACIALIS
a form of Iris
*BENDS OVER UNTIL ITS BLOOM
TOUCHES THE GROUND*
-AND THEN TAKES ROOT A STEP
AWAY FROM THE MOTHER PLANT

*VALMONT
SONIAT* DUFOSSAT
WHO WAS A PLANTER IN
NEW ORLEANS IN THE 1840's
*IS REMEMBERED IN THAT
CITY BY STREETS BEARING
EACH OF HIS 3 NAMES*

THE LANTERN COFFEE POT

USED IN ENGLAND IN 1692 HAD GLASS INSETS SO THAT WHEN IT WAS NOT BEING USED TO BREW COFFEE *IT COULD SERVE AS A LANTERN*

ROBERT E. CRADDOCK

of Warren County, Ky., A VETERAN OF THE AMERICAN REVOLUTION AROSE FROM HIS DEATHBED UNASSISTED, DONNED HIS UNIFORM AND HAD A PIPER AND DRUMMER MARCH AROUND HIS HOME *—SO HE COULD ENJOY HIS OLD REGIMENTAL MARCHES AS THE LAST SOUNDS HE WOULD HEAR ON EARTH* (1837)

SHETLAND ISLAND SHEEP
ARE NOT SHORN *THEIR WOOL IS PLUCKED OUT*

KING'S HOUSE
in Spanish Town, Jamaica,
SINCE IT WAS SWEPT
BY A FIRE IN 1927
*ACTUALLY IS ONLY
A PORTICOED FAÇADE*

A BRIDE
in the oasis of Siwa,
Africa,
MUST WEAR
A SWORD
DURING HER
WEDDING
CEREMONY

THE EGGS
of the flatheaded
catfish of
Brazil
ARE HATCHED
IN CUP-LIKE
CELLS
*OUTSIDE
ITS STOMACH*

"VOS OMNES"
AN ANCIENT ROMAN
EXPRESSION MEANING
"YOU ALL"

JOHN MYTTON
(1796-1834)
of Halston, England,
CURED HIMSELF OF
HICCOUGHING
**BY SETTING FIRE
TO HIS NIGHTSHIRT!**
*HE HAD A NARROW
ESCAPE FROM DEATH—BUT
IT CURED HIS HICCOUGHS*

THE **SIMPLEST CENSUS IN HISTORY**
Persia, KNOWING THAT EACH OF ITS CITIZENS
CONSUMED ONE LOAF OF BREAD A DAY,
FOR CENTURIES ESTIMATED ITS POPULATION
MERELY BY **COUNTING THE NUMBER
OF LOAVES SOLD IN THE COUNTRY**

KATHERYN TUDOR
(1535-1591) of Berain, Wales,
ACCEPTED 2 PROPOSALS OF
MARRIAGE IN 1566 DURING THE
FUNERAL OF HER 1st HUSBAND

MAURICE WYNNE BECAME HER 2nd
HUSBAND AND WHEN HE DIED IN
1570 SHE MARRIED SIR RICHARD
CLOUGH—HAVING ASSURED HIM AT
THE GRAVE OF HER FIRST HUSBAND
**THAT SHE WOULD MARRY
HIM AFTER THE DEATH OF
HER SECOND SPOUSE!**

*SHE ALSO BURIED SIR RICHARD
AND IN 1580 TOOK EDWARD
THELWALL AS HER 4th HUSBAND*

THE
IRON CLUB
WEIGHING **2 POUNDS**

WITH WHICH
APPRENTICES WERE
CHASTISED IN THE
LABOR GUILDS
OF EUROPE

*WAS OFFICIALLY
CERTIFIED —AND
CALLED "JUSTICE"*

AN **ORNAMENTAL BELT**
WORN BY SHILLUK TRIBESMEN
of the White Nile, in Africa,
*CONSISTS OF THIN
DISKS MADE FROM
THE SHELLS OF
OSTRICH EGGS*

JUSTICE PHILIP J. McCOOK of New York

WAS A CORPORAL IN THE SPANISH-AMERICAN WAR, A MAJOR IN WORLD WAR I *AND WAS MADE A COLONEL IN WORLD WAR II AT THE AGE OF 69*

THE **MARKET** of Antigua, Guatemala, IS LOCATED IN THE RUINS OF AN OLD CHURCH

NEPHILA MACULATA A GIANT SPIDER OF INDIA, EXUDES AN OIL FROM ITS SALIVARY GLANDS *TO KEEP FROM GETTING STUCK IN ITS OWN WEB*

OYSTER SHELLS
ARE USED IN THE WEST
CAROLINE ISLANDS
IN THE PACIFIC
AS MONEY

FOOTMEN
AT THE ROYAL CASTLE
of Amalienborg, Denmark,
WEAR AS PART OF THEIR
ORNATE HEADGEAR
*POTS FILLED WITH
ARTIFICIAL FLOWERS*

ROBERT QUIRKE, KEEPING A
VOW MADE WHEN HIS SHIP WAS
IN DANGER OF FOUNDERING IN
THE BAY OF BISCAY, SCRAPPED
THE VESSEL ON HIS SAFE
RETURN TO MINEHEAD, ENGLAND,
AND USED ITS LUMBER TO BUILD
*11 ALMSHOUSES –WHICH ARE
STILL STANDING 333 YEARS LATER*

"DACHSHUND" SHEEP
DEVELOPED BY A BREEDER
in Oslo, Norway,
*HAVE SHORT LEGS
AND LONG BODIES*

STEVE McCANN
of Eau Claire, Wis.,
WHO ENLISTED IN THE UNION
ARMY DURING THE CIVIL WAR
SERVED IN THE 1ST
WISCONSIN REGIMENT
WITH 7 OF HIS SONS
AND 2 SONS-IN-LAW

SEWARD V. COFFIN
(1867 - 1948)
of Middletown, Conn.,
VACATIONED AT THE
SAME HOTEL AT
BLUE MOUNTAIN
LAKE, NEW YORK.

EVERY SUMMER
FOR 70
YEARS

A BARREL OF WINE WAS ROLLED BY
2 GERMANS NAMED PUETZ and MAINZER
FROM BERNKASTEL TO BERLIN
– A DISTANCE OF 500 MILES

135

THE **OLDEST CUSTOM HOUSE IN THE U.S.**
Newport, R.I.,
ESTABLISHED IN 1682

THE **"FLICKER FISH"** of Tahiti

ARE BANDED BLACK AND WHITE – A CAMOUFLAGE THAT MAKES THEM APPEAR TO BE JUST *A FLICKER OF LIGHT AND SHADOW ON THE WATER*

HAS WINGS 5 TIMES AS LONG AS ITS BODY

The **LONG-WINGED MOTH** of Argentina
(Copiopteryx virgo)

THE **HIPPOPOTAMUS** HAS A STOMACH **10 FEET LONG**

THE STONE OWL
NATURAL ROCK FORMATION
Blue Mountains of Jamaica

THE LADY GUARDIAN OF THE RAVINE OF DALUIS
France
NATURAL STONE FORMATION

THE **"Y" BRIDGE**
Lyons Falls, N.Y.

THE **LEAD ROOF**
of Temple Church,
in London, England,
MELTING IN A FIRE
DURING THE LONDON
BLITZ ON MAY 10, 1941,
FLOWED TO THE FLOOR
OF THE SANCTUARY
AND THEN COOLED
IN THE SHAPE OF
THE BRITISH LION
—*EMBLEM OF THE
NATION'S SPIRIT
OF DEFIANCE*

BASKETS
ARE WOVEN
FROM THE
**BURITI
PALM**
BY THE
**BAKAIRI
INDIANS**
of Brazil
*IN LESS
THAN 10
MINUTES*

137

POTATO VALENTINE
Submitted by
BYRON TRASTER
Fairmount, Ind.

THE JAIL
In Niagara Falls, Canada, BUILT IN 1817, HAD CELLS WITH NO WINDOWS AND NO HEAT FOR CRIMINALS, *BUT THOSE FOR DEBTORS HAD BOTH WINDOWS AND FIREPLACES*

SPIES
IN THE MEXICAN WAR OF 1847-48 WERE INSTANTLY IDENTIFIABLE *BECAUSE THEY WORE A PRESCRIBED MILITARY UNIFORM*

THE PARCHMENT WORM
BUILDS A U-SHAPED TUBE AT THE BOTTOM OF THE SEA, THEN PUMPS WATER THROUGH THIS NEST *SO IT CAN FEED UPON THE MICROSCOPIC CREATURES OF THE SEA*

138

A TURNIP IN THE SHAPE OF A SHRIVELED HAND IS REGARDED BY GERMAN FARMERS AS A SIGN THAT THEY WILL HAVE POOR CROPS

ALEXANDER THE GREAT
HAD ONE BLACK EYE AND ONE BLUE EYE

DANIEL DURBIN
of Seattle, Wash.,
HIS MOTHER, MRS. MARGARET BROWN DURBIN, AND HIS GRANDFATHER, HAROLD BROWN, ALL WERE BORN ON JULY 12TH

A WASHING MACHINE
SOLD IN THE U.S. IN THE 1800's, WAS MOUNTED ON ROCKING-CHAIR LEGS SO THE CLOTHING COULD BE ROCKED CLEAN

HENRY CAVENDISH

(1731-1810) THE ENGLISH CHEMIST AND PHYSICIST, WAS SO SHY IN THE PRESENCE OF WOMEN THAT HE BUILT A SEPARATE STAIRCASE IN HIS HOME *THAT THE HOUSEMAIDS WERE FORBIDDEN TO USE*

HERMAN MARCUS

of Vicksburg, Miss., PLAYING GOLF AT THE VICKSBURG COUNTRY CLUB IN 1937, SHOT A HOLE-IN-ONE ON THE SECOND HOLE

-AND SCORED ANOTHER HOLE-IN-ONE 25 YEARS LATER ON THE SAME HOLE

LEATHER WINE BOTTLES

in medieval times

WERE SHAPED LIKE THE ANIMALS FROM WHOSE PELTS THE BOTTLES WERE MADE

ARTHUR RIMBAUD (1854-1891)

CELEBRATED FRENCH POET, ENTERED COLLEGE AT *THE AGE OF 10*

THE SHIVA TEMPLE
of Utterkashi, India,
WAS BUILT TO ENSHRINE AN
ANCIENT PILLAR OF METAL
26 FEET HIGH
**BECAUSE IT HAS MYSTERIOUSLY
REMAINED FREE OF RUST**
FOR 2,400 YEARS

CAN A
MAGNET
PICK UP
A U.S.
COIN?

(Answer
tomorrow)

ROCK
WITH A
PERFECT
OUTLINE
OF THE
NUMBER
1
Submitted by
MIKE THOMPSON,
Glendive,
Montana

Emperor **ALEXANDER I**
of Russia
ONCE SUFFERED A HEADACHE
THAT COST **#10,000,000!**

THE COURT DOCTOR ORDERED CANDLES SO
THE EMPEROR COULD INHALE THEIR SMOKE--
BUT **91** YEARS LATER **4,000,000** TAPERS
WERE FOUND IN THE PALACE--BECAUSE NO
ONE HAD CANCELLED THE **DAILY DELIVERY**
OF CANDLES!

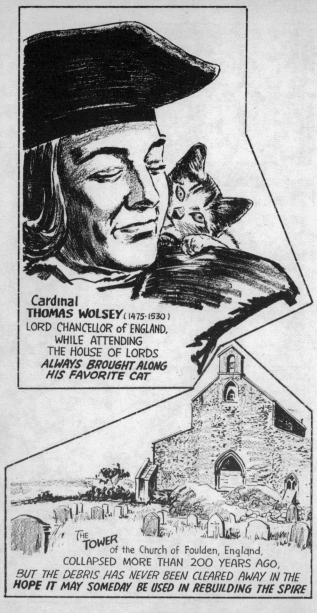

Cardinal **THOMAS WOLSEY** (1475-1530)
LORD CHANCELLOR of ENGLAND,
WHILE ATTENDING
THE HOUSE OF LORDS
*ALWAYS BROUGHT ALONG
HIS FAVORITE CAT*

THE **TOWER** of the Church of Foulden, England,
COLLAPSED MORE THAN 200 YEARS AGO,
*BUT THE DEBRIS HAS NEVER BEEN CLEARED AWAY IN THE
HOPE IT MAY SOMEDAY BE USED IN REBUILDING THE SPIRE*

142

THE MEMORIALS TO 8 MISTAKES!
.Gumbum, Mongolia,

8 LAMAS TRICKED INTO ATTENDING A CONFERENCE WITH A CHINESE GENERAL, WERE EACH ASKED IF HE COULD PREDICT **THE DAY ON WHICH HE WOULD DIE**

THE FRIGHTENED LAMAS ALL REPLIED "TOMORROW," BUT THEY WERE BEHEADED THAT VERY DAY

–AND 8 WHITE TOWERS NOW STAND ON THE SITE OF THEIR EXECUTION TO COMMEMORATE THEIR ERROR

THE TOWER of the Parish Church in Ashwell, England, BUILT BY THOMAS EVERARD 248 YEARS AGO, CARRIES ON ITS ROOF THIS INSCRIPTION: "Thomas Everard placed me here, He said to last a hundred year"

GRAPE VINES ON ROANOKE ISLAND, N.C. *ARE MORE THAN* **300 YEARS OLD**

3 WHITE COWS
ARE GIVEN ANNUALLY BY THE
SHEPHERDS of Baratous, France,
TO THOSE of Roncal, Spain,
*AS PAYMENT TO THE
SPANISH SHEPHERDS FOR
HAVING PERMITTED BARATOUS
TO BECOME PART OF FRANCE*
587 YEARS AGO

THE **COUNT de CUSTINE**
of France,
WHO BECAME FAMOUS AS
"GENERAL MUSTACHE" WHILE
SERVING IN THE AMERICAN
REVOLUTION, HAD ENTERED THE
FRENCH ARMY AS A LIEUTENANT
AT THE AGE OF 7

THE **FIRST MAIL-ORDER HOUSE**
A ONE-ROOM HOUSE,
PREFABRICATED IN CHICAGO, ILL,
WAS ADVERTISED IN AN 1870
CATALOGUE FOR **$175**

THE **GIANT
CRAB-EATING
FROG**
SWALLOWS
CRABS IN
THEIR SHELLS

THE TEMPLE of HEAVEN
in Peking, China, INCLUDED AN ALTAR SO SACRED THAT FOR *CENTURIES ONLY THE CHINESE EMPEROR COULD STAND ON IT*

THE BIRTHPLACE of the TELEPHONE
ALEXANDER GRAHAM BELL CONDUCTED HIS EXPERIMENTS ON THE TOP FLOOR OF THE BUILDING AT 109 COURT ST., IN BOSTON, MASS., AND *IN 1875 FIRST SUCCEEDED IN TRANSMITTING SPEECH BY ELECTRICITY*

THE BATHS at Tambo Machay, Peru,
BUILT OF GRANITE BLOCKS BY THE INCAS, WAS CONSTRUCTED WITHOUT MORTAR, YET THE ROCKS FIT SO TIGHTLY THAT A KNIFE BLADE CANNOT BE **INSERTED BETWEEN THEM**

The **Earl of Angus** (1489-1557) AS A BOY FELL IN LOVE WITH QUEEN MARGARET of Scotland, SISTER OF KING HENRY VIII, **AND WHEN HE GREW UP MARRIED 3 MARGARETS IN SUCCESSION** -HIS SECOND WIFE BEING QUEEN MARGARET HERSELF, WHO HAD BECOME A WIDOW IN 1513

THE **GOLDEN DOMES OF KADIMAIN** Bagdad THE CUPOLAS OF THIS MOSQUE ARE COVERED WITH SHEETS OF **SOLID GOLD ONE INCH THICK AND VALUED AT $1,300,000!**

A LOG CABIN ON TILICUM ISLAND, PA., BUILT BY SWEDISH SETTLERS IN 1650, *IS STILL USABLE 326 YEARS LATER*

THE
10ᵀᴴ EARL
OF
DUNDONALD
1775-1860
A BRITISH ADMIRAL,
CREATED A SECRET WEAPON WHICH SO
HORRIFIED THE ADMIRALTY THAT
**HIS INVENTION WAS ORDERED
SEALED FROM VIEW FOREVER**

*55 YEARS AFTER THE ADMIRAL'S DEATH
WINSTON CHURCHILL BROKE THE SEAL AND
LEARNED THE INVENTION WAS POISON GAS*
**- BUT THE GERMANS WERE
ALREADY USING IT**

A **HINDU PAGODA** in Madura, India,
THAT IS TOPPED BY A CHRISTIAN CROSS
IT I'S ONE OF 17 SUCH CHURCHES IN INDIA THAT SERVE THE
ASHRAM BROTHERHOOD, A HINDU CHRISTIAN SECT

IRON BELLS CARRIED IN THE AFRICAN CONGO BY THE FOLLOWERS OF A NATIVE PRINCE AS THE SYMBOL OF HIS AUTHORITY

JOSEPH STALIN (1879-1953) THE SOVIET RULER, TO RAISE MONEY FOR THE MARXIST CAUSE, AS A YOUTH, *WAS A BANK ROBBER*

THE MONKEY-EATING EAGLE WHICH FEEDS ON MONKEYS AND LARGE BIRDS, *IS FOUND ONLY IN THE PHILIPPINES*

THE GROUND CUCKOO
CAN RUN AS FAST AS A RACEHORSE

ELEVATORS
IN DEPARTMENT STORES
IN THE LATE 1800's WERE
ORNATELY DECORATED
AND FURNISHED
*WITH SEATS FOR
PASSENGERS*

John **PARRY**
famed 18th-
century harpist,
WAS THE BEST CHECKERS
PLAYER IN ALL WALES
-YET HE WAS TOTALLY BLIND

HORSES WERE SOLD
in Australia in 1924
FOR ONE CENT EACH

THE LEAF FISH
SWIMMING HEAD DOWN, LOOKS LIKE A DRY, BROWN LEAF DRIFTING IN THE WATER

ELIAS HOWE
(1819-1867) of Spencer, Mass., INVENTOR OF THE SEWING MACHINE, HAVING GONE TO ENGLAND IN AN ATTEMPT TO GET FINANCIAL BACKING, BECAME SO IMPOVERISHED THAT TO PAY HIS PASSAGE HOME, **HE PAWNED HIS MODEL AND PATENT PAPERS**

A **MONUMENT** IN KINHASA, THE CONGO, COMMEMORATING THE INTRODUCTION OF THE RAILROAD, DEPICTS *THE HUMAN CARRIERS WHO FORMERLY TRANSPORTED ALL CARGOES*

THE **MOTMOT** of Mexico ALWAYS RIPS BIG GAPS IN ITS TAIL FEATHERS

MRS. **OLIVE WALKER** OF WORPLESDON, SURREY, ENGLAND, A GRANDMOTHER, WAS THE VILLAGE'S *CHIMNEY SWEEP*

THE CASTLE A MAN BUILT TO ESCAPE HIS SHADOW
Puxerloch, Austria

CHARLOT a knight of Charlemagne, CONSTRUCTED A FORTRESS IN A CAVE AND LEFT IT ONLY ON MOONLESS NIGHTS *SO HIS SHADOW COULD NEVER PURSUE HIM*

LEATHERJACKET

THE FISH THAT CAN'T BE SCALED. ITS SCALES ARE SET AT VARIOUS ANGLES

TABLE ROCK

NATURAL FORMATION. THAT STOOD FOR YEARS IN LINCOLN COUNTY, KANSAS

THE **TETHYS** IN A PERIOD OF 4 MONTHS, LAYS **478,000,000 EGGS**

THE **MISTAKE THAT SAVED A CITY!** *THE MANGIA TOWER,* in Siena, Italy, WAS NAMED FOR ITS FIRST BELLRINGER, WHO RANG THE BELLS BY ERROR IN 1348 —AROUSING THE TOWNSPEOPLE JUST IN TIME TO FIGHT OFF A MIDNIGHT ATTACK

THE 'FROZEN' WATERFALL
THE CAVE OF GARGAS, NEAR
Saint-Bertrand-de-Comminges, France
A MASS OF STALACTITES

DANIEL ANTHONY
BROTHER OF
SUSAN B.
ANTHONY, THE
SUFFRAGETTE,
HIMSELF A
CONTROVERSIAL
EDITOR OF THE
LEAVENWORTH,
KANSAS,
"CONSERVATIVE,"
*WAS SHOT AT
5 TIMES,
BEATEN AND
HORSEWHIPPED
AT THE AGE
OF 67*

FRENCHMEN
IN THE
1780'S WORE
THEIR HAIR, OR
WIGS, PATTERNED
*AFTER THE
HEDGEHOG*

153

THE LARGEST BEEHIVE IN THE WORLD

BEE ROCK NEAR Sublimity Springs, Laurel County, Ky., ONCE HOUSED SO MANY BEES THAT WHEN THEY FLEW AWAY IN SEARCH OF NECTAR *THEY DARKENED THE SKY*

AN **ANCIENT GRAVE MARKER** CARVED BY ROMANS, VISIBLE IN THE WALL OF THE PARISH CHURCH OF HIRSAU, GERMANY

WILLIAM HENRY HARRISON PORTRAYED BY HIS FOLLOWERS AS A PLOW-PUSHING MAN OF THE PEOPLE IN THE U.S. PRESIDENTIAL CAMPAIGN OF 1840 -- *ACTUALLY WAS A WEALTHY VIRGINIA PLANTER*

4-LEGGED CHICKEN
Submitted by MRS. HILTON TORREYSON, Tompkinsville, Md.

JOHANN PETER LYSER
(1803-1870) of Germany
WAS CELEBRATED AS A PAINTER, POET, MUSICIAN AND MUSIC CRITIC IN DRESDEN, VIENNA AND BERLIN FOR 33 YEARS
-YET THROUGHOUT THAT ENTIRE PERIOD HE WAS TOTALLY **DEAF**

THE CATHEDRAL OF SAINT-MALO
France
CONDEMNED DURING THE FRENCH REVOLUTION, WAS SOLD TO A FISHERMAN ON HIS PLEDGE TO
REDUCE IT TO RUBBLE!
KNOWING THE CHURCH COULD NOT BE HARMED WITHOUT ITS OWNER'S SANCTION -ITS PURCHASER VANISHED AND WAS NEVER SEEN AGAIN!

THE STAY-AT-HOME BIRD
THE NIHOE MILLERBIRD IS FOUND NOWHERE IN THE WORLD EXCEPT ON THE 146 ACRES OF NIHOA, HAWAII

THE ELM TREE GRAVE
Catherine de Bogart of Woodstock, N.Y., DIED AS A RESULT OF A BEATING AND WAS BURIED STILL GRASPING THE ELM TREE SWITCH

–WHICH GREW INTO A HUGE TREE THAT FORCED ITS WAY UP THROUGH HER GRAVESTONE

DR. HIPOLITO IRIGOYEN
(1850-1933)
RE-ELECTED PRESIDENT OF ARGENTINA IN 1928, AFTER HAVING BEEN OUT OF OFFICE FOR 6 YEARS, REFUSED TO MOVE INTO THE PRESIDENTIAL PALACE––
LIVING INSTEAD IN AN APARTMENT OVER A STORE

A FORD RUNABOUT IN 1923 *SOLD FOR $265*

The Rev.
Thomas
LINDLEY

WAS
CURATE OF
HALTON GILL,
England,

**FOR 70
YEARS**

DR. ALICE HAMILTON
IN 1919 BECAME THE FIRST WOMAN
ADMITTED TO HARVARD'S FACULTY
*BECAUSE SHE WAS THE ONLY PERSON
IN THE COUNTRY QUALIFIED TO TEACH
HER SUBJECT--INDUSTRIAL MEDICINE*

The Rev. T.J.
ZUMWALT
WAS AN
*ITINERANT
PREACHER
IN THE
OZARKS FROM
1860 TO 1927
--A PERIOD
OF 67
YEARS*

DACHSHUNDS
ARE NOT GERMAN
*THEY WERE
KNOWN IN
EGYPT IN
2,000 B.C.*

A DECLARATION OF INDEPENDENCE

STATING:" that all the acts of the British Parliament tending to take away Rights of Freedom ought not to be obeyed " **WAS ADOPTED BY THE CITIZENS OF CHESTER, VERMONT, ON OCTOBER 10, 1774**

THE **GUILLOTINE** WAS NAMED FOR JOSEPH I. GUILLOTIN (1738-1814), WHO DID NOT INVENT IT, AND WHO RECOMMENDED ITS USE IN THE FRENCH REVOLUTION ONLY BECAUSE IT WAS MORE MERCIFUL THAN *THE SWORD AND NOOSE*

THE **AUK** - A SWIMMING BIRD, *CAN DIVE TO A DEPTH OF 60 FEET*

EDWARD PREBLE (1761-1807) AN AMERICAN NAVAL OFFICER WHO BOMBED THE BARBARY PIRATES AT TRIPOLI, UPON LEARNING THAT ALL THE OFFICERS ASSIGNED HIM WERE UNDER 30, PROTESTED: "THEY HAVE GIVEN ME NOTHING BUT A PACK OF BOYS!"

THE **SAW FISH**
THE BICHIR, A FRESHWATER FISH OF AFRICA, HAS ON ITS BACK A SERIES OF FINLETS THAT WHEN UPRIGHT LOOK LIKE **THE TEETH OF A SAW**

GRADUATES of VASSAR ORIGINALLY RECEIVED ONLY CERTIFICATES OF "*THE FIRST DEGREE OF LIBERAL ARTS*" BECAUSE IT WAS CONSIDERED UNSEEMLY FOR A WOMAN TO BE CALLED A BACHELOR OF ARTS

LHASA THE CAPITAL OF TIBET, ON SUMMER DAYS REGISTERS 90 DEGREES AT NOON-- *AND ZERO AT MIDNIGHT*

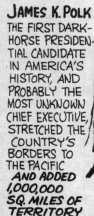

JAMES K. POLK THE FIRST DARK-HORSE PRESIDENTIAL CANDIDATE IN AMERICA'S HISTORY, AND PROBABLY THE MOST UNKNOWN CHIEF EXECUTIVE, STRETCHED THE COUNTRY'S BORDERS TO THE PACIFIC *AND ADDED 1,000,000 SQ. MILES OF TERRITORY*

THE **TREE FROG** WHICH HAS SUCKERS ON ITS TOES, CAN HANG UPSIDE DOWN FROM TREE LIMBS

SIAMESE CANTALOUPES
Submitted by Thomas D'Amico, Jr., Milwaukee, Wis.

LON CHANEY
STARRED IN " LONDON AFTER MIDNIGHT," IN 1927 -- THE FIRST VAMPIRE FILM MADE IN AMERICA

A **MAPLE LEAF** **MEASURING 12"× 12"** found by Mrs. Franth Wetherholts, Mattoon, Illinois

A **STATUE**
OF GEORGE WASHINGTON
WAS MOVED FROM THE EAST LAWN OF THE CAPITOL
IN WASHINGTON, D.C., IN 1908, BECAUSE THE PUBLIC
*WAS OFFENDED BY THE NUDITY DISPLAYED
BY ITS GRECIAN GOD ATTIRE*

A **STARFISH
SHELL**

WITH A WATCH
IN ITS CENTER IS
USED FOR PROPHECIES
in Mrewa, Mashonaland,
Africa,
BY A WITCH DOCTOR
WHO BELIEVES IN
KEEPING UP WITH THE TIMES

THE SERPENTINE A SNAKE-SHAPED MUSICAL INSTRUMENT WAS USED IN ORCHESTRAS IN COLONIAL AMERICA IN THE 18th CENTURY

SEPP AN ALSATIAN DOG OWNED BY FERDINAND HATZINGER OF MUNICH, GERMANY, **COULD BALANCE ON HIS NOSE A COFFEE SERVICE FOR FOUR**

ROBERT COATES (1772-1848) A BRITISH ACTOR, OFTEN REWROTE SHAKESPEARE'S PLAYS TO SUIT *HIS OWN TALENTS*

A **BOY** of the TURKANA TRIBE, Africa

BEFORE ENGAGING IN THE ANNUAL TRIBAL DANCE

PAINTS A CAGE OVER HIS FACE

USED & DONE FOR

CANCELLATION STAMP
USED BY THE POSTMASTER OF FAIRHAVEN, CONN.
IN 1851

CHICK WITH **3** LEGS
Owned by Merlin and Marvin Greese, of Metairie, La.

THE CAVE-LIKE OPENINGS
IN THE ROCKY CRAG OVERLOOKING THE GOREME VALLEY, ASIA MINOR, *ARE ACTUALLY CHURCHES CARVED IN THE STONE IN THE EARLY DAYS OF CHRISTIANITY*

THE ALLIGATOR GAR of the Southern United States
HAS NOT CHANGED IN 300,000,000 YEARS.

THE **ELABORATE FLORAL DESIGN**
WHICH DECORATES THE CITY
HALL PLAZA IN OROTAVA IN
THE CANARY ISLANDS FOR THE
FESTIVAL OF CORPUS CHRISTI,
IS CREATED SOLELY FROM
EARTH OF DIFFERENT COLORS

A **BELL** In Uppsala, Sweden,
HAS BEEN RUNG TWICE EACH
DAY SINCE 1597 AS A MEMORIAL
TO THE WOMAN WHO CAST IT
-*THE WIFE OF KING JOHN III*

A **MAGNET**
CAN PICK
UP ONLY ONE
ISSUE OF
U.S. COIN –
*THE "WHITE" CENT
OF 1943, WHICH
CONTAINS IRON*
Submitted by JACK REED
Scottsdale, Arizona

THE
**INDIAN
HEAD**
SO. GATEWAY
ROCK,
COLORADO
SPRINGS, COLO.
*NATURAL
STONE
FORMATION*

WOOD MARKED WITH **A PERFECT STAR**
Submitted by CEISTA LITTLE, Detroit, Mich.

KING SAHALE SELASSIE of Shoa, Ethiopia, CELEBRATED EACH NEW YEAR'S *BY PERSONALLY PAYING THE DEBTS OF EVERY PAUPER IN HIS KINGDOM*

ELBURS, A TOWN ON THE SLOPE of Mount Elburs, in Iran, IS SO CONSTRUCTED THAT THE ROOFS OF HOUSES ON ONE LEVEL *SERVE AS THE STREET FOR THE NEXT HIGHER ROW OF HOMES*

THE FERRY
CARRYING WORSHIPERS TO JAPAN'S MIYAJIMA SHRINE, HAS A PROW *RESEMBLING A FIERCE DRAGON*

DANIEL WEBSTER (1782-1852)
WAS A BITTER FOE OF JOHN C. CALHOUN ON THE ISSUE OF SLAVERY, BUT WHEN CALHOUN DIED IN 1850, WEBSTER *DELIVERED THE EULOGY*

NAPOLEON'S HAT
IN THE FICHTEL MOUNTAINS of Germany
A GIANT ROCKING STONE THAT LOOKS LIKE A COCKED HAT
-AND ALSO SHAKES SIDEWAYS AND NODS UP AND DOWN

Kitten
EATS CORN ON THE COB
Submitted by
THOMAS CARMICHAEL
Metairie, La.

A **RAILROAD** in Stephansort, Papua, *IS POWERED BY OXEN*

SIEVING THE BABY

AN ANCIENT TRADITION IN THE DAKHLA OASIS OF THE LIBYAN DESERT, *INVOLVES SHAKING EACH 7-DAY-OLD BABY IN A LARGE SIEVE WITH A PINCH OF SALT AND A LITTLE WHEAT, BARLEY AND RICE.* THE GRAIN THAT FALLS TO THE GROUND IS ALLOWED TO BLOW AWAY IN THE BELIEF IT WILL ASSURE A GOOD LIFE TO THE CHILD WHEREVER HE MAY TRAVEL IN THE FUTURE

THE **ARCH OF TRIUMPH** in Barcelona, Spain, WAS ORIGINALLY CONSTRUCTED AS *THE ENTRANCE GATE TO THE BARCELONA FAIR IN 1888*

THE FIRE FLOWER
(Epilobium Augustifolium)
ONLY GROWS ON SOIL
SEARED BY FIRE

JUDGE JOHN G. WILKIN

(1818-1889) of Middletown, N.Y.,
WHO PRACTICED LAW FOR 36 YEARS,
WAS SO SUSPICIOUS OF WOMEN THAT
HE NEVER REPRESENTED ONE IN COURT
*AND REFUSED TO PARTICIPATE
IN ANY TRANSACTION IN WHICH
A WOMAN WAS INVOLVED*

THE **TOMB** of Harispe
CHIEF of East Nigeria, Africa, IS
ADORNED BY A TABLEAU DEPICTING
THE CHIEF SEATED ON HIS THRONE
—AND UPHELD BY THE
*COMMANDER OF HIS ARMED FORCES
AND HIS PRIME MINISTER*

WINE DELIVERIES TO ANCIENT BABYLON WERE MADE VIA THE EUPHRATES RIVER *IN ROUND BOATS THAT ALWAYS CARRIED A DONKEY—*

AT BABYLON THE BOATS WERE SOLD BECAUSE THEY COULD NOT BE PROPELLED UPRIVER AGAINST THE CURRENT— AND THE TRIP HOME WAS MADE ON THE DONKEY

PROLOGUE CAMPOS of Pará, Brazil, *HAD 3 BROTHERS NAMED* **CHAPTER, ERRORS** and **EPILOGUE**

THE **SANS SOUCI HOUSE** IN Siasconset, Mass., WAS ORIGINALLY PART OF A TWINE FACTORY. ITS KITCHEN WAS A BOAT HOUSE, AND ITS BRICKS WERE THE BALLAST ON A WRECKED SHIP

WOOD CRATES
WERE USED AS BALLOT BOXES
IN NEBRASKA IN 1871, BUT
IN ONE ELECTION A CROOKED
OFFICIAL WAS SPOTTED
STUFFING FAKE BALLOTS
THROUGH A KNOTHOLE

OFFICIALS
IN THE DUTCH EAST INDIES
SHOWED THEIR RANK BY
*THE NUMBER OF RINGS
ON THE UMBRELLA THAT
SHIELDED THEM FROM
THE SUN*

**THE CHURCH OF SAN LORENZO
IN MIRANDA**, Rome,
WAS BUILT INSIDE THE COLUMNS OF
AN ANCIENT PAGAN TEMPLE ERECTED
BY EMPEROR ANTONINUS PIUS
1,800 YEARS AGO

THE **STATE CAPITOL**
OF OHIO, AT
COLUMBUS,
BECAUSE OF
FINANCIAL AND
LABOR TROUBLES
AND A CHOLERA
EPIDEMIC, WAS
NOT COMPLETED
*UNTIL 20 YEARS
AFTER ITS CORNER-
STONE WAS LAID*

CALF
OWNED BY DAN
MARTIN OF
BELLE PLAINE, IA.,
BORN ON
THE **7**th
DAY OF
THE **7**th
MONTH
WITH A
PERFECT
7 ON ITS
FOREHEAD.

Submitted
by Chester
P. Fredericks
Chicago, Ill.

JAN TARNOWSKI
POLISH STATESMAN, HAD 5 SONS
*AND NAMED EVERY ONE
OF THEM JAN*

TRIBESMEN OF Baluchistan, Pakistan, WEAR TROUSERS MADE FROM **40 YARDS OF CLOTH**

"TIGER" A DOG OWNED BY CHRISTINE ALBERT, *SHELLS AND EATS INDIAN NUTS* Maspeth, N.Y.

THE **WILLIAM PENN STATUE** ATOP THE CITY HALL OF PHILADELPHIA, PA., 37 FEET HIGH AND WEIGHING **53,348** LBS., IS *THE LARGEST SCULPTURE ON ANY BUILDING IN THE WORLD*

173

THE TEMPLE OF TARISI
Tibet

IS ROOFED WITH SOLID-GOLD TILES
VALUED TODAY AT $173,250!

THE CHURCH BUILT OF SNOW

William Kraut
of Enzweihingen, Germany,
AT THE AGE OF 8
**BUILT A 25-PEW
CHURCH OF SNOW**

THE BIRCH LEAF ROLLER

PROVIDES A
CONTAINER FOR ITS
EGGS AND FOOD
FOR THE EMERGING
LARVA BY MAKING
EXACT INCISIONS
IN A BIRCH LEAF
*AND THEN ROLLING
IT TO FORM AN
INGENIOUS CONE*

AN **ICE-CREAM MACHINE**
BOUGHT IN 1784 BY
GEORGE WASHINGTON

A **MARRIED WOMAN**
of the Sudan
WEARS HER GOLD
WEDDING RING
IN HER NOSE

The **GROTTO** OF THE
ANNUNCIATION
in the Franciscan
Monastery in
Washington, D.C.,
IS SO FAITHFUL A
COPY OF THE CHAPEL
in Nazareth, Israel,
*THAT IT HAS EVEN
REPRODUCED
EXACTLY A COLUMN
FROM WHICH A
PIECE WAS CUT
OUT BY ROBBERS
WHO INVADED THE
ORIGINAL CHAPEL
IN 1638 SEEKING
HIDDEN TREASURE*

The **STATUE WITHOUT A FACE**
Kyrene, Libya,
A STATUE ERECTED TO HONOR
HIS WIFE, BY AN ANCIENT ROMAN
*WHO FELT SHE WAS SO
BEAUTIFUL, NO SCULPTURED
FACE WOULD DO HER JUSTICE*

A **SINGLE PARAMECIUM**
ONLY 1/125TH OF
AN INCH LONG
*COULD IN 5 YEARS
PRODUCE A MASS
OF OFFSPRING
FILLING AN AREA*
**10,000 TIMES THE
SIZE OF THE EARTH**

The **TREES** IN FRONT OF
The Potala Palace of the
Dalai Lama of Tibet
HAVE BEEN SO TWISTED BY
THE VIOLENT WINDS THEY
LOOK LIKE CORKSCREWS

The **LANTERN FLY**
of Dutch Guiana
IS NOT A FLY AND
CASTS NO LIGHT—
*IT IS A BUG, AND THE
"LANTERN" PROTRUDING FROM
ITS HEAD IS ALWAYS DARK*

HORSE CARTS in Mongolia ARE CONSTRUCTED *WITHOUT A SINGLE NAIL*

A **SCOLD'S BRIDLE** USED ON NAGGING WOMEN IN 17th-CENTURY GERMANY, WAS AN IRON MASK *WITH A BIT THAT HELD THE TONGUE STILL AND A BELL THAT RANG IF THE WEARER MOVED HER HEAD*

THE LOTTERY OF DEATH!
George Bibb Crittenden
1812 - 1880

ONE OF THE TEXANS FORCED BY THEIR MEXICAN CAPTORS TO DRAW LOTS TO DETERMINE WHICH WOULD DIE, SELECTED A LUCKY WHITE BEAN —BUT GAVE IT TO A FELLOW PRISONER WHO HAD A WIFE AND CHILDREN

HE DREW AGAIN FOR HIS OWN FATE —AND AGAIN PICKED A WHITE BEAN
1843

A GAME BOARD FOUND BY A HARVARD EXPEDITION IN IRELAND, HAD BEEN CARVED OUT OF YEW WOOD *IN THE 10TH CENTURY*

WAI WAI TRIBESMEN OF BRITISH GUIANA AND BRAZIL THRUST 2 SCARLET MACAW FEATHERS THROUGH THE SEPTUM OF THEIR NOSE --TO LOOK *LIKE HANDLEBAR MOUSTACHES*

A WINDMILL THAT ONCE STOOD IN THE CENTER OF LAS VEGAS, N.M., WAS TORN DOWN IN 1880 IN THE BELIEF THE WATER IN ITS WELL HAD BEEN CONTAMINATED BECAUSE *SO MANY MEN HAD BEEN HUNG FROM IT*

A **MOTHER OPOSSUM** AFTER HER BABIES ARE LARGE ENOUGH TO LEAVE HER POUCH, *CARRIES THEM AROUND ON HER BACK*

WHEN MEN WERE MEN
MEN IN AMERICA IN THE 1700's, HAVING SHAVED THEIR HEADS TO ACCOMMODATE THE PERIOD'S HOT WIGS, USUALLY WORE TURBANS INDOORS AND *SLEPT IN NEGLIGEE CAPS*

THE FIRST HOMES
BUILT BY THE PILGRIMS AND PURITANS IN AMERICA *WERE WIGWAMS MADE OF BARK, THATCH AND WATTLES DAUBED WITH MUD*

A WIDE TURBAN
IS DONNED BY WOMEN OF SZECHWAN, CHINA,
IN THE BELIEF IT WILL **CURE A HEADACHE**

A **ROMAN PIPE ORGAN**
IN THE AQUINCUM MUSEUM
IN BUDAPEST, HUNGARY,
*IS PLAYABLE AFTER
2,000 YEARS*

ROLLER SKATES

ADVERTISED
IN LONDON,
ENGLAND,
IN THE 1800's,
WERE
ACTUALLY
*SMALL
TRICYCLES*

THE LUCKIEST GIRLS IN THE WORLD!

A GIRL of the LENGUA TRIBE of Bolivia CAN CHOOSE AS HER HUSBAND ANY BACHELOR IN THE TRIBE *-AND HE CAN'T SAY NO!*

THE TOWN HALL

OF NORTH SALEM, N.Y., BUILT IN 1773 AS A MANOR HOUSE, *HAS ALSO SERVED AS AN ACADEMY, COURTHOUSE AND JAIL*

THE **KAPELL BRIDGE** at Lucerne, Switzerland, WAS CONSTRUCTED **643** YEARS AGO

181

THE MANOR OF BENTLEY STILL STANDING ON STATEN ISLAND, N.Y, WAS THE SITE OF *THE FIRST PEACE CONFERENCE IN AMERICA* LORD HOWE, COMMANDER OF THE BRITISH FORCES, MET BENJAMIN FRANKLIN, JOHN ADAMS AND EDWARD RUTLEDGE HERE IN 1776

ADDISON PITT AN ACTOR FROM LONDON, ENGLAND, SPOKE THE LAST LINES UTTERED ON THE STAGE OF FAMOUS OLD MACAULEY'S THEATER IN LOUISVILLE, KY.

HALF A CENTURY EARLIER, THE FIRST LINES SPOKEN IN THAT THEATER WERE *DELIVERED BY PITT'S ACTRESS MOTHER, FANNY ADDISON*

A WALKING-STICK CAMERA INVENTED BY A. LEHMANN of Berlin, Germany, IN 1903

THE **AYE-AYE** FOUND ONLY IN MADAGASCAR, IS EQUIPPED WITH A LONG MIDDLE FINGER THAT ENABLES IT TO DIG GRUBS OUT OF TREES

ROY ACUFF

THE TENNESSEAN CALLED THE FATHER OF COUNTRY MUSIC, HAD PLANNED TO BE A PROFESSIONAL BASEBALL PLAYER--*BUT HIS BALL CAREER ENDED ABRUPTLY DURING SUMMER TRAINING WITH THE YANKEES WHEN HE SUFFERED A SUNSTROKE*

THE **CATHEDRAL** OF **NOTRE DAME** IN REIMS, FRANCE, WAS STARTED IN 1211 AND COMPLETED IN 1430 *--219 YEARS LATER*

TANKARDS AND **TABLEWARE** USED BY THE COLONISTS AT PLYMOUTH WERE ALMOST ENTIRELY WOODEN

THE OLDEST PRINTED MAP A MAP OF WESTERN CHINA SHOWING PART OF THE GREAT WALL --PRINTED IN 1155

ANTOINE de la Mothe **CADILLAC** (1656-1730) THE FRENCH SOLDIER WHO FOUNDED DETROIT, MICH. WHO WAS COURAGEOUS AND WITTY, BUT HAD A VERY LONG NOSE, *INSPIRED EDMOND ROSTAND'S* "CYRANO de BERGERAC"

RINSING BOWLS WERE A SOCIAL NECESSITY IN COLONIAL AMERICA SINCE MANY WINES WERE SERVED *AND THE GLASSES HAD TO BE RINSED BETWEEN EACH CHANGE OF WINE*

THE **KAGU BIRD** OF NEW CALEDONIA, WHICH IS FLIGHTLESS, HAS A VOICE THAT SOUNDS LIKE A PUPPY DOG

A **TRAVELING TRUNK** OFFERED FOR SALE IN WOLVERHAMPTON, ENGLAND, IN THE 1800's, CONVERTED INTO A *BATHTUB*

MRS. ENOS BROWN OF TRAVER HOLLOW, N.Y., WAS FAMED IN THE LATE 19th CENTURY AS A **BEAR HUNTER**

HUGE LAND CRABS in Cuba, *CAN OUTRACE A HORSE*

The **IBIS** IS CONSIDERED SO SACRED BY THE OSIRIS CULT of EGYPT THAT A SPECIAL CEMETERY HALF A MILE SQUARE WAS ESTABLISHED AT ABYDOS, EGYPT, FOR MUMMIES OF THESE WINGED COURIERS OF THE GODS

EUGLENA VIRIDIS A MINUTE WATER ORGANISM CALLED THE PUPIL OF THE EYE *CONSTANTLY CHANGES ITS SHAPE*

The **BOERS** RECRUITED AT THE START OF THE BOER WAR AGAINST THE BRITISH IN 1899, WERE *SUBJECT TO SERVICE FROM 16 TO 65, WORE THEIR OWN CLOTHING, CARRIED THEIR OWN RIFLES, AND WERE NOT PAID*

The **ZEBRA FISH** OF THE INDIAN OCEAN HAS ZEBRA-LIKE STRIPES

THE **OLDEST BRICK PAGODA** IN CHINA

THE BUDDHIST TEMPLE OF SUNG-YUEH SSU AT SUNG SHAN, HONAN, WHICH HAS 12 SIDES AND 15 STORIES, WAS BUILT OF BRICK **453 YEARS AGO**

GEORGE TAYLOR OF EASTON, PA., ONE OF THE SIGNERS OF THE DECLARATION OF INDEPENDENCE, *CAME TO AMERICA AS AN INDENTURED SERVANT*

A **WATCH CAMERA** PATENTED BY M. NIELL IN 1903, TOOK PICTURES THROUGH ITS STEM

A **LIGHTHOUSE** BUILT BY THE ROMANS AT BOULOGNE ON THE NORTH COAST OF FRANCE, SERVED AS A WARNING TO SHIPS AT SEA *FOR 1,400 YEARS*

M̲R̲S̲ **EDITH BOLLING GALT WILSON**
THE WIFE OF PRES. WOODROW WILSON, VIRTUALLY RAN THE COUNTRY DURING HER HUSBAND'S LONG ILLNESS--*YET* **SHE OPPOSED FEMALE SUFFRAGE**

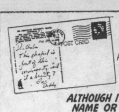

POST CARD MAILED FROM Princeton, N.J., AND DELIVERED TO CHARLES A. KEARNS of Wayne, N.J.

ALTHOUGH IT CARRIED NO NAME OR ADDRESS

The **NAME** of the **LAST KING OF KAFFA** Africa

WAS KNOWN TO ONLY **7 PEOPLE** —

THE SEVEN DIGNITARIES GAVE THE MONARCH THE NAME GAKI SHEROTSKO — *AND KEPT IT SECRET IN THE BELIEF THE KING COULD NOT BE HARMED BY ANYONE WHO DIDN'T KNOW HIS NAME*

THORSTEIN VEBLEN (1857-1929) POLITICAL ECONOMIST, SOCIOLOGIST AND SOCIAL CRITIC, WHO WAS BORN AND REARED IN A NORWEGIAN COMMUNITY IN WISCONSIN, *SPOKE NO ENGLISH UNTIL HE WENT TO COLLEGE*

THE BEACHES
of Patagonia, in So. America,
ARE COVERED AFTER
HIGH TIDE WITH
*MILLIONS OF SARDINES
AND OTHER FISH*

THE 10th **EARL of COVENTRY**
(1838 - 1930)
HELD HIS TITLE FOR
86 YEARS

THE **CHURCH OF LE PLANÈS**
In France
ORIGINALLY WAS CONSTRUCTED
AS THE TOMB OF AN ARAB
REBEL NAMED MUNAZA WHO
WAS EXECUTED DURING A
MOORISH INVASION
OF FRANCE IN 721

MAJOR JOHN DYKE ACLAND
A BRITISH MILITARY OFFICER,
WHO FOUGHT AGAINST THE
COLONIES IN THE AMERICAN
REVOLUTION, WAS SEVERELY
WOUNDED AND MADE A PRISONER
-- YET UPON HIS RETURN
TO ENGLAND HE FOUGHT
A DUEL WITH ANOTHER
BRITISH OFFICER WHO HAD
MALIGNED THE AMERICANS

A **BABY OSTRICH**
IS A FOOT HIGH AT
BIRTH, AND DURING THE
NEXT 6 MONTHS GROWS
A FOOT EACH MONTH

**ONE OF THE
LANTERNS**
PLACED IN
BOSTON'S OLD
NORTH CHURCH
IN 1775, AS A
SIGNAL TO PAUL
REVERE, IS
STILL IN WORK-
ABLE CONDITION

THE WANTON-LYMAN-HAZARD HOUSE BUILT IN NEWPORT, R.I., IN 1675, IS THE *OLDEST HOUSE IN NEWPORT*

Sir HARRY LAUDER (1870-1950) WHO BECAME WORLD FAMOUS FOR HIS SONGS IN SCOTTISH DIALECT, LAUNCHED HIS PROFESSIONAL CAREER *SINGING AN IRISH SONG*

MARBLEHEAD LIGHTHOUSE BUILT ON MARBLEHEAD PENINSULA IN 1821, *IS THE OLDEST LIGHTHOUSE IN OHIO*